GOD Guns & Gays

Why OBAMA is DANGEROUS For America

Author: Freddie L. Woodley III

God Guns & Gays
Why Obama Is Dangerous for America

By: Freddie L. Woodley III

For my Grandma Joan whose footprints were often the only ones in the sand.

This book is also dedicated to my loving mother Marilyn and my darling wife Sucre...

TABLE OF CONTENTS

INTRODUCTION

rev·o·lu·tion
[rev-uh-loo-shun]

noun

1. an overthrow or repudiation and the thorough replacement of an established government or political system by the people governed.

2. *Sociology.* A radical and pervasive change in society and the social structure, especially one made suddenly and often accompanied by violence. Compare social evolution.

There have been many sequential events leading up to where we are today in terms of our culture, politics and the overall social order of our commonwealth. Events have the power to affect our lives on an individual basis or move us collectively as a nation. They have the ability to test our faith, challenge our resolve, and in some cases, determine our fate. Some believe that the future has been predetermined for us through a divine order of Biblical past events. Others believe that our destiny is yet to be determined and is much like a never ending story that can be told and retold as often as we'd like for it to be— that the actions we take today are merely precursors to the events that will shape our lives tomorrow. The latter implies that we can control our destiny, alter the course of time, and forge our own way. I am a strong believer in forging one's own way. When I was a young man, I left home and sacrificed everything I had in order to carve out a path for myself, so I recognize when I see others who are determined to do the same. Upon Obama's first appointment as president of the United States, it became apparent to me that our nation had changed direction. Not only did Americans overwhelmingly vote for the most unlikely of candidates, but in doing so sent a powerful message to the establishment that the people of America collectively believe in forging their own way.

The election of Barack Obama brought with it many things. It rendered an undeniable sense of pride and accomplishment for blacks who had sacrificed so much during the slave and Civil Rights eras. It gave many whites a sense of absolution for the transgressions of their ancestors against blacks. However, it also hardened the hearts of those who see white supremacy and traditional white leadership as the single, most picturesque view of America.

Obama represents a paradigm shift in American politics and culture. His appointment has revealed a fundamental change in how we see ourselves working together in order to meet our challenges, tackle common goals, and divvy up the pie at the end of the day. He embodies what will be remembered in history as a time of great change in our nation's history.

Social change doesn't happen inside of a bubble – it's not an isolated event. It can begin with something as simple as an idea that sparks a flame in the thought process of a person or group people. The result is a form of enlightenment within a small subset of the social community with the potential to spread like wildfire. For example, in the 17th and 18th century, Europe underwent a transformation of thought when a group of scholars decided they were fed up with society wandering around in the intellectual wilderness. Up until that point, mankind believed wholly in superstitions, mystical philosophies, and rationale based upon unscientific data. The scholars, led by such intellectuals as Spinoza, Isaac Newton, John Locke, and Voltaire, believed they could reform society by using reason and faith-based principles to challenge Ideas. They also believed they could expand the knowledge-base of mankind through the *Scientific Method*. This period became known as the *European Enlightenment* or *Age of Reason* within European history. It has been noted that the American Revolution was closely tied to the enlightenment of Europe. Some scholars insist the American Revolution was directly influenced by the events that were shaping European society at the time and was thus dubbed the period of American Enlightenment.

In essence, a spark ignited in Europe that eventually spread around the world. This spark en kindled great changes in the political, social and intellectual landscape of America. It is much like the changes taking place in the global society today. Information travels fast in today's world. Young people are like data receptacles that are constantly being bombarded with information. They share their world with people of various races, origins, and backgrounds. If there's a social injustice taking place anywhere on the planet, it becomes viral in a matter of minutes resulting in young people being extremely acute when it comes to issues that potentially affect them or their friends around the world. These days a spark can be ignited by a tweet or a photo shared on MySpace, stirring a conversation in the blogosphere and raising consciousness by the tens of thousands in an instant.

If we were to re-examine the manner in which Americans voted in 2008 we'd have to come to terms with the reality of the results. The result of the people's choice was a drastic change from traditional politics and a new standard for how we choose our nation's leaders moving forward. People began asking, "How did this happen?" The answer is quite simple; when presented with the right information, The American public was able to make an informed decision about who they wanted to lead them. The diffusion of proper information was the key to mobilizing America's youth and making them excited about the potential of their participation within the voting process and potentially shattering the glass ceiling in Washington. It was a youth- led revolt against traditional governance and politics as usual coupled alongside a coalition of voters to which traditional Republican principals either ostracized or failed to appeal to. In Barack Obama they saw someone that appealed to their innermost desires and self interests. They felt comfortable with his leadership and trusting enough to grant him the power to take us to a new place in America and alter the course of history.

CHAPTER 1

Health Care Woes

"Americas healthcare system is neither healthy, caring, nor a system."
-Walter Cronkite

On March 23, 2010 Barack Obama signed one of his most courageous and signature achievements into law. The Patient Protection and Affordable Care Act (PPACA) or the newly coined Obama-care, became one the most talked about pieces of health care legislation since the introduction of Medicare and Medicaid in the mid 1960's. With a number of goals in its sights, the Affordable Care Act aims directly at decreasing the number of uninsured Americans and reducing the overall cost of insurance coverage. It streamlines the delivery of healthcare by accurately updating patient records and providing individuals with a means to acquire a primary care physician, thus encouraging pre-emptive doctor visits and keeping non-emergency individuals out of emergency rooms. Perhaps most important, it prohibits insurance companies from discriminating against those with pre-existing conditions or dropping individuals in the event they get sick.

Members of Congress have battled over the issue of health care for years asking —"What is reform and how do we implement it?" The task always seemed monumental and there was no doubt that if a plan truly came forward and was put into effect, it would shake up a lot of people. But that wasn't the only thing keeping law makers from tackling the burden of healthcare inadequacies in this country. We mustn't forget about the influence big insurance companies have within Washington and the stranglehold lobbyists continue to have over many members of congress.

These days it takes a person of significant will power and altruism to put the interest of the people above payoffs from big insurance groups. Why can't we just go back to the days when information was privileged and people didn't know they were dying from cigarette smoke or that America is the most obese nation in the world? Law makers wish for this kind of naïve thinking on the part of the people every day. If that were indeed the case, resolving health care issues would be much simpler right? Of course… but therein lies the problem, **too much information**. The more people become informed about their diminishing quality of life, the more they want their government to do something about it. The status quo of a bunch of fat cats on Capitol Hill enjoying the best insurance coverage that money can buy while their constituents suffer with menial, or in some cases no insurance, becomes no longer acceptable.

Joe Biden said it best because It truly is "…a BIG EFF'in Deal!" when **ALL** Americans have access to health care, especially when those who stand to benefit the most from this legislation are the poor (of all races), blacks, and Hispanics and women. The CDC says that: "Insurance coverage is directly related to better health outcomes and in contrast the uninsured rates for blacks and Hispanics is significantly higher when compared to whites, Asians and Pacific Islanders." Those families with median incomes under $50,000 suffer egregiously from a lack of health care insurance and typically use the emergency rooms for all of their health care related issues.

It is a fact that black men and women age 45-74 have much higher death rates from Coronary Heart Disease (CHD) than any other race. Black women in particular died at a higher rate of (37.9%) over white women (19.4%) before the age of 75 as a result of

CHD. Black men also die at a rate of (61.5%) over white males (41.5%) due to CHD. The statistics are virtually identical when the effects of stroke are examined as well. Blacks and Latin-Americans are also much more prone to obesity than whites. Half of all Latino children born in America since 2000 are at risk for diabetes. High rates of diabetes due to heredity and obesity can be directly linked to ethnicity. Lack of health care as well as other socioeconomic disparities between these two groups further exacerbates the issue of health related complications and premature death.

Our government's established poverty line is $2,050.00 for family of four. The number of impoverished families from all ethnic backgrounds rose from 14.3% to 15.1% according to data released by the U.S. Census Bureau on September 13, 2011. It currently stands at its highest rate since 1993 when Bill Clinton succeeded George Bush Sr. as president of the United States. When individual families face economic disparities of this magnitude, and one of its members gets sick, it is hard and sometimes impossible to recover. The sick family member, usually an adult, refuses medical attention and runs the risk of turning a curable illness into a potential death sentence. Children go unseen by a physician and as a last resort are brought into the E.R. at the guardian's expense. Some rely on spiritual reckoning or faith to relieve them of their woes. Others simply have no idea where to turn.

To the 15% of Americans living in poverty P.P.A.C.A. is a game changer. New regulations would give poor families an opportunity to address health related issues as they come about, thus ending the cycle of procrastination and latent medical attention. Routine doctor visits and pre-screening provide early detection of potential life threatening diseases. The Affordable Health Care Act aims at keeping our children healthier by leveling the playing field for health care access and will lead the charge in the fight against malnourishment and onset diabetes. As a result of the new law children will have the opportunity to live healthier lives and good health will permeate well into their educational performances and overall well being.

What kind of message does a man send to those watching him when he can't be bribed by the interest of big insurance companies? How much of champion for the poor and other minorities does he become when he puts their needs ahead of his own? How do those who have sold out to corporate lobbyist stand in contrast to a man who refuses to? Perhaps if more conservatives were to follow the example of Chief Justice Roberts, who in my opinion, went against the will of his own party and stood up against the Right Wing bully machine at a crucial moment in our nation's history, we'd have a better nation of policy makers. Unfortunately Republicans have pushed unyieldingly to destroy Obama-care while making no apologies all the while. They are determined to disqualify Barack Obama's achievement on passing health care, by pushing legislation and filing legal claims, all in an effort to destroy the bill, but have yet to put forward a single plan of their own to replace it. Even if one was to disagree with the bill as it exists today, considering what it does for the poor and middle class families, it would be logical to improve upon the legislation rather than scrap the whole thing and go back to the system we had in place before its passage. But those who aren't concerned with being righteous concern themselves only with evil deeds and de-legitimizing the presidency of Barack Obama. They remain part of an elitist group of men that hold fast to a belief system, much like their forefathers, that intelligent men of color are a threat to their existence. Their only interest is perpetuating a subtle form of the same war on black America that their predecessors waged under the biased hand of J. Edgar Hoover and many others in the 1960's to disqualify any outspoken leaders within the black community.

Why are conservatives white men so opposed to health care reform? Could it be that with access to health care black men and women would live healthier, longer lives? Or that Latin Americans would recover from being the most uninsured group in the U.S. to a fully insured thriving community? Maybe they're opposed to the idea that all children who are born predisposed to diabetes can no longer be denied coverage under Obama's new law? Honestly, I don't know what they fear. But what I do know is that we are a nation founded upon Christian principles. The bible teaches us that: "…What so ever you have done for the least of these brothers and sisters of mine, ye have did for me." (Mathew 25:40) When those who profess to be god fearing people of good moral character and decency abandon the principles that their faith in God and country is founded upon, they in essence become the true definition of a hypocrite. They leave the people of whom they are chosen to lead with no other alternative than to look upon them with shameful disdain and repugnance. This is what's truly sickening about the American health care system. Obama's resolve on this issue alone forces us to look inward at how we care for the sick, elderly, and poor in this nation. However, there are those who would much rather see the poorest among us suffer unnecessarily in order to avoid reform and any potential de-funding from lobbyist backlash and that is *Dangerous for America.*

CHAPTER 2

Fiscal Terrorist

"Competition has been shown to be useful up to a certain point and no further, but cooperation, which is the thing we must strive for today, begins where competition leaves off."
-Franklin D. Roosevelt

"Everybody's worried about stopping terrorism. Well there's a really easy way; stop participating in it."
-Noam Chomsky

In 1929 the U.S. stock market crashed and directly impacted industrialized nations around the world. Soon after the world economy collapsed and brought with it a host of unprecedented issues. With 25% of Americans out of work the political landscape underwent a drastic change, Herbert Hoover loss re-election by an overwhelming majority to Franklin Delano Roosevelt (FDR). Along with FDR came big ideas and huge policies for putting Americans back to work, policies which became coined as The New Deal. With it came great power and upward mobility for the Democratic Party. It made them the majority in which they (Dems) would hold the white house for the next seven out of nine presidential terms.

Roosevelt had proposed a series of government sponsored programs aimed at relief, recovery, and reform which became known as the 3 R's. In summary the R's would provide relief for the impoverished, recovery from the depression, and Reform of the U.S. banking institutions. It strengthened the labor unions and like a defibrillator, jolted our nation's economic vitals back to life. Since then, FDR's New Deal has been a model for success and the cornerstone of discussion during times of economic downturn.

In contrast, George W. Bush provided us with 8 years of executive leadership during which time he so graciously gave us the Iraq War, Bush era tax cuts, and the worst economic conditions in U.S. history since the Great Depression. Upon Bush's exit from the white house the U.S. unemployment rate was at a substantial 7.8 % with 12,049,000 people claiming they were unemployed. In January of 2009 Bush conceded the presidency to Barack Obama and left the white house. I can only imagine the feeling of relief that came over him as he passed the baton to the newly elected statesman. "Here you go Mr. President, the mess is all yours now… Laura, girls, let's get the hell outta here! The unemployment rate continued to rise to a staggering 10% during the first few months of Barack's presidency, also at which time, towards the end of October, Senator Mitch McConnell addressed his party with the declaration that the conservative party's number one goal was to make Barack Obama a 1 term-president. He also said during the briefing— *"We need to be honest with the public. This election is about them, not us. We need to treat this election as the first step in retaking the government. We need to say to everyone on Election Day, Those of you who helped make this a good day, you need to go out and help us finish the job."* Despite inheriting a rapidly increasing unemployment rate and much to the dismay of those opposed to Barack's position of power in the White House, the numbers on the economy have and continue to improve. So far in spite of republican opposition, the president's policies have given us 30 straight months of private sector job growth and 25 months of public sector growth.

Mitch McConnell's statement was a declaration of war against the president. And because the president was chosen overwhelmingly by the will of the people, it was also a declaration of war upon the citizens of this nation. Mitch McConnell, Eric Cantor, and the entire Republican Party, on that day, vowed that they would make no concessions toward the president or his policies no matter what the cost. Even if that cost meant a slower than necessary economic rebound, continued high unemployment percentages, and denying millions of Americans health care coverage. He and his cronies are directly responsible for the stagnation in our nation economic recovery. They have held the American people hostage as a protest against their choice to put a black man in charge of the white house. Like a gang of thugs they have used scare tactics, lies, and intimidation to filibuster everyone of the president's job generating proposals and like a fierce constrictor, the GOP continues to squeeze the life out of our nation's work force in an all out effort to incapacitate and ultimately devour our laborers. A perfect example of this is the fight over our nation's debt ceiling lead by the Republican's in the spring of 2012. John Boehner, the speaker of the house and Tea Party puppet, along with other members of the House announced in May, which coincidentally was the middle of the election year, they would not vote to allow a raise in the debt ceiling unless serious cuts to spending were added. In other words- we're not going to do what has traditionally been a *no brainer* unless we get to look like we're calling the shots to our party constituents.

Historically leaders in congress have never opposed raising the debt ceiling as doing so could have detrimental effects on our nation's global credit rating. The president warned Boehner that he would not allow Congress to hold the nation's economy hostage. Boehner scoffed back at the president insisting that- "As long as I'm around I'm not going to allow the debt ceiling to be raised without doing something about the debt." Let us keep in mind that it was Boehner's previous boss George W. Bush that ran up the deficit in the first place. The previous summer's ego fest had already left the U.S. with a lowered credit rating from Standard & Poor's (An American finance company that publishes research and analysis on stock and bonds). Ultimately a deal was struck between the President and Boehner that provided a temporary fix, putting the issue aside until after the election when the debt ceiling would need to be addressed again. As Republicans anxiously awaited poll numbers on Election Day that would hopefully signify Obama's defeat, they were met with astonishing proof of Obama's coalition of support around the nation. But did John Boehner learn or take away any lessons from the people's decision? The answer is a resounding NO! Immediately after the election members of the House lead by speaker Boehner, dug in and used their political capitol to once again, protect the nation's top 2% from tax increases as negotiations resumed in order to avoid the fiscal cliff. More than a month after the election our political leaders in Washington had failed to move the needle in either direction in terms of avoiding financial disaster and speaker Boehner is in the center of it all.

I believe it's time to ask Speaker Boehner just who do you work for? Might he and Mitch McConnell be on some corporate payroll? Could there be any other reason for a member of congress to lobby so aggressively for the nation's top income earners? The polls have shown consistently for months that the majority of Americans both Democrat and Republicans are in favor of some tax increase on the nation's wealthiest to a tune of some 76%. Polls also show that the majority of Americans would blame the Republicans if the country goes over budget. It's only common sense when you have a member of congress fighting tooth and nail to protect the richest individuals in the country, against the overwhelming desire of the people to do just the opposite, that he stands to lose something if not a great deal if he were to fold during these kind of negotiations? Or could it simply be that Boehner and Mitch McConnell are exactly the kind of men of weak character that they themselves accuse this president of being? Are they the kind of men who have no influence over their own party members? Has all their years in congress afforded them no political clout on Capitol Hill? Are we to believe the influence of the newly established Tea Party is so strong to where negotiations begin and end at their foothold? Or has the politics of this nation changed so much that gerrymandering now controls the house and senate to the degree that most of our elected officials are from districts that have no interest in bipartisan politics in the first place, so there's no incentive to compromise?

Republicans know that if Barack Obama is successful at turning around the nation's current economic crisis using similar tactics to FDR's government sponsored work programs and incentives, what would soon follow is a wave of Democratic majority leadership and dominance for years to come. They are determined to prevent this at all cost, even at the detriment of their own party and like suicide bombers, strap each other down with extremist views, hateful rhetoric, and bigoted venom before hurling themselves onto the house floor and national media coverage to detonate with explosive furry over the issues of the day. They bomb on issues of women's rights. They bomb on issues of social welfare. They bomb on practically every issue relevant to the American public yet in the eyes of their constituents they become martyrs.

The premise behind the Tea Party and Republicans use of obstructionist tactics against the president's policies is the notion that Obama equals bigger government. It's a rally against the institution that F.D.R. successfully employed to bring this country back from economic disaster in the earlier 1930's. The question then becomes, if not government sponsored programs, then what…private sector? Are we honestly to believe that private corporations care about the condition of the nation's infrastructure, educating our children, welfare of the poor or anything else other than profit? Show me a corporation with a moral compass and I'll show you a crack head that tithes. Somehow the political right is able to brainwash its base into believing that it is best to allow Wall Street to go unregulated and Big Banks to go unchecked. Through the National Rifle Association (NRA) and many other Right Wing conservative groups they have convinced the rebel son's of this nation that the Obama Administration has come to take away their guns and do so in the name of big government. They have played on the emotions of groups like the Tea Party and Birthers, using them to further their agenda and it's sad…

The problem with balancing the economic system is that there is too much demand as a result of over population and too much greed. Barack's position of fairness to all people doesn't coincide with the Republican position of *by your own boot straps,* herein the conflict lays. Republicans have shown us over the last few years just how deep the relationship between big corporations and wealthy investors goes and their philosophy is simple— What good is a nation of people who don't use their intelligence? G.O.P. Elites don't believe the public is responsible enough to make choice economic decisions so they work tirelessly to keep the bulk of the nation's wealth out of the hands of the undisciplined many and well into the hands of the self disciplined few. Lobbying for tax breaks for the nation's top tier 2% is necessary for those members of congress, with whom they've become bedfellows, to indulge in order reap the benefits of the corrupt corporate agendas. They are motivated by greed and place value upon their lives in terms of the amount of dollars they are able to rake in on the backs of middle class Americans. Barack's message threatens that relationship by asking the corporations, that many members in congress lobby for, to pay more in taxes, where in some cases they are paying very little if not any at all. This position of leveling the tax code would drastically affect lobbyist ability to earn income and further fuels their disdain for Obama.

Mitt Romney, the former presidential challenger to Obama, insisted that one of his key qualifications for being president was that he knows how the economy works. There is a big difference in knowing how the economy works and knowing how *Robber Barons,* like Romney would prefer that it work. The way it works right now is that the nation's top income earners, which are about 2% of the U.S. population, control nearly 40% of the nation's wealth. They do so by manipulating tax codes and loop holes to prevent paying taxes on earned income and then hoard American dollars into offshore accounts, which in my opinion is the most unpatriotic thing any righteous American could do. To add further to their lack of patriotism, they then refuse to reinvest those dollars back into the U.S. economy because the American worker demands a cost for his labor 5x's that of his Chinese counterpart. Those who maintain these types of financial practices only believe that the economy works best when they have control over the majority of the nation's wealth as they argue that the rest of us are too incompetent to manage the nation's economy. This is the basis of Trickle down *Economics*. It's a philosophy which says- *"Give us all of your money, for we are the elite; we are the ones best suited to determine what is good for the direction of this country and after we make the best investments for the nation, that we deem appropriate, then by our grace alone you may eat."* But this is not the way the economy flourishes. Model after model has shown us that top down economics doesn't work. What truly fuels an economy is demand for goods and services. The mere notion that businesses do better when they have more money to hire more people or produce more goods is a reverse psychology aimed at tricking the people into supply side economics. The truth is that a company may well produce more goods but it does them no good when those products sit idle on the shelf or in a warehouse. Furthermore, business owners don't hire people because they have more tax breaks; they hire people when demand for their services triggers a need for increased productivity. In other words people have to have the discretionary income necessary and ready available in order to purchase the goods a company produces and the companies are then forced to hire in order to keep up with the demand. You must strengthen the middle class. This is accomplished by lessening the tax burden on middle class families, cracking down on predatory lending, and by not incentivizing companies to take American jobs overseas. This is how the economy truly grows- from the *Middle Out.*

We hear our political leaders say quite often that we need to have an open and honest discussion in this country... The response is yes, indeed we do. So tell us honestly Mr. McConnell, just who you are referring to when you use the term "Them" when referencing who the election of Barack Obama was about? And who are you so adamant about taking the government back from? Although he would deny it, the underlying message of his speech is that, we (white superior males) have an obligation to take this country back from the welfare niggers, boarder jumpers, gays, and liberals.

Today our country faces enormous economic challenges. The previous administration under Bush no doubt ran our economy into a ditch. Mitch McConnell and his cronies are willing to drive the economy even further, maybe even off a cliff in order to push their extreme Right Wing agenda. It is sociopathic behavior at its essence. The willingness to hold the economy hostage or the willingness to veto government sponsored work programs that strengthen our nation's infrastructure is detrimental and genocidal.

It would appear that the semblance of Barack Obama brings out the worst in men like McConnell and Cantor. I used the word sociopath to describe their behavior because intellectual men of this caliber know better. When leaders of men set aside good judgment and behave in an amoral fashion in order to promote a wicked agenda, they consciously refuse to do what is in the best interest of the people they've been chosen to represent. Ultimately they become led by their egos and big heads get in the way of huge progress and that is Dangerous for America.

CHAPTER 3

The Gag Reflex

"I would remind you that extremism in the defense of liberty is no vice! And let me remind you also that moderation in the pursuit of justice is no virtue!"
-Barry Goldwater

During a recent doctors visit I found myself engaged in a mutual conversation with my physician about Obama and his policies. Doc likes to talk politics while the meter runs up a tab on my vehicle parked outside. I don't mind having these discussions with him as I find his points of view interesting and helpful in supporting my argument that today's Right Wingers are the most extreme group of Conservatives to exist in modern times. Doc is a white male Republican and a bit of a slouch. In fact the first time I met him he was in worse shape than I was. But that's alright with me (the fact that he's a slouch) because besides his political viewpoint he's very honest and straightforward. He was going on about how he was going to quit practicing medicine if Obama-care wasn't repealed. Of course I asked him to explain his position, to which he informed me that under Obama-care, regulations would require that he adhere to certain protocols. The example he gave was a scenario where on one hand there's a black 50 year old male with diagnosed diabetes and on the other hand there's a 39 year old white woman with a diagnosed heart condition. For reasons he did not clearly explain, the 50 year old black male would be given a priority number of 1 and the female would be given a lower priority number of 2. He claimed that Obama-care would force him to treat the patient with the higher priority number before treating the patient with the lower priority number. In a nutshell, he would no longer be able to practice medicine open and freely. My immediate response was - "Where is that written in the bill...I need to see documents?" Telling me something based on fact is one thing but blowing a bunch of smoke in my direction because it's the general consensus amongst he and his peers while they share a drink at the bar is another. He insisted that it was in the bill and would provide me with proof sooner than later. I'm still waiting... Furthermore, it was not a legitimate enough argument against all of the positive things that reform provides. What harm is there in following a few protocols (doing something your government asks of you) if it saves lives? Irrespective of the individual perks of Obama-care, which poll after poll shows Americans overwhelmingly like or agree on, the arguments against it are solely aimed at the fact that its government oriented. The truth of the matter is that private sector organizations are not interested in the welfare of the people. Private firms are only interested in profit. The overall welfare of the state and its people cannot be left up to private interest groups who with no moral compass, make decisions solely on the basis of net profits and capital gains.

We began to discuss other things like how much of a hypocrite he felt the president was for proceeding with the 2nd T.A.R.P. bailout which the Bush Administration had initiated. He criticized Obama for condemning Bush's initial T.A.R.P. handout, only to go back and provide the banks with a second handout himself during his first few months in office. Doc's position was that Obama should not have provided any form of bailout to either the banks or the auto industry. His contention was that they all should have been allowed to fail. Let the whole system collapse and then perhaps things would right themselves when the privileged elite have a taste of what the everyday man on Main Street faces. I told him that he'd obviously never been hit over the head with the butt of a gun while walking to and from his Mercedes by the proverbial everyday man on Main Street who's down on his luck.

People who have been victims of violent crimes tend not to be tolerant of situations that yield violent behavior. I felt compelled to tell him that no sitting president wants the collapse of the entire nation's economy on his conscience— that neither Bush nor Obama could let that happen without taking measures to prevent it. How would it look, especially during the term of the first African American president, to have the entire nation's economy roll off the cliff on his watch? Not to mention the other nations affected either directly or indirectly by the stability of the U.S. economy. In an effort to find some common ground on the subject, I shared with him my feelings on black pride in America and how much of that seemed to have been lost (in my opinion). I further expressed that during the civil rights movement, blacks had been so deprived of the most basic of things that would constitute a descent living, when we were finally granted access to voting rights, equal housing, and integration we had evolved a sense of pride in our selves and communities for all that we sacrificed in order to get it. It was nothing to go through a black neighborhood and see well kept homes, manicured lawns, and dignified people walking about and sharing with their neighbors. Over time, as generations proceeded, the more privileged we became the more future generations felt entitled to things our ancestors fought and bled for without having to make the same sacrifices. I agreed with him that if you deprive the human spirit of a thing long enough, it will develop a sense of ownership and an overwhelming need to protect that which it has been yearning for once it eventually acquires it. America has been, and for now, continues to be one of the richest countries in the world. Her children are like the children of the black community I alleged to have lost some self regard along the way.

Collectively we have lost that sense of pride that once was the core fabric of our nation. Made in the U.S.A. doesn't carry the same weight that it used to. Perhaps it's because we don't see enough of it, or maybe even more so because we are no longer the leaders of the industrialized world. What are we doing as a nation that others might want to emulate? Were no longer leaders in car manufacturing, nor are we the great pioneers in space exploration we once were. The race to build the world's tallest skyscrapers and the steel industry have all become trivialized by the ability of other countries to reach the same heights if not higher or even produce at the same rates if not more. Somewhere America has to throw down the gauntlet and challenge the world to reach for new heights and break new barriers.

America has become a nation of outsourcing and in the opinion of this writer, *outsourcing* is unpatriotic. Profit can never take precedent over loyalty to ones country and greed has no home in the heart of a patriot. How many vacation homes does one need? How many private jets? At what point does a company CEO place core values over dollar value? Perhaps when he too becomes deprived and has to struggle like the common man does today? But this is no equitable remedy for the ills that plague our society. Doc's proposal to let the bottom fall out of society is an *extreme* position and a dangerous one indeed. Unfortunately he's part of a much larger group of individuals who share the same extremist viewpoint which is; *let it all go to hell* or *kill everything in sight* AND THEN- *let it all go to hell!*

The world is a different place now. Everyday citizens have access to mass killing weapons and the fine line between fantasy and reality, for them grows thinner every day. I suggested to him that killers like Jared Laughner and James Holmes are merely symptomatic examples of where we are as a society in terms of our coping skills and that extreme viewpoints, like the one he and many other conservative extremists share, don't fully take into account the affect their resolve has on those struggling to maintain a grip with reality- those unstable individuals who internalize the anger expressed by their political leaders and then act out in the most heinous of fashions in retribution against society. You can ask any victim of an extremely violent crime in which chaos has ensued, if they agree with allowing society to fall into mass chaos and they will emphatically tell you- NO! Someone has to be the steward of common sense and the wielder of the gavel of justice and order. That order must be maintained for the sake of those innocent lives caught in the middle of extremist backlash against government expropriation. Our communities are not battlefields nor should they become one in order to persuade greedy corporate outsourcers to patriotically keep jobs on U.S. soil. I told Doc that his manner of thinking was irresponsible. I also told him that handing Mitt Romney the presidency would be equivalent to rewarding criminal behavior, which I'll explain more in depth later on in this book.

The extremist of today has to come to grips with the true reason for their resentment of the Federal government. They who quickly point the finger and lay blame at the foot of government when in fact it has been the leaders of the private sector screwing over working class Americans for the last 20 – 30 years. They have done so by outsourcing jobs for the sake of gaining huge profits and as a result have effectively reduced the overall GNP and GDP of the entire Nation. Helping to facilitate all of this was the Bush policies that hinged greatly upon the concepts of personal responsibility, economic freedom, and property ownership, (Ownership Society). There's no doubt these are three virtuous concepts indeed however the glue that binds them all together in this equation is **personal responsibility** and although economic freedom and the right to own property are fundamental ideas, the idea of personal responsibility is more complex.

Personal Responsibility is a relative concept based upon the individual or in some cases, a group of individuals who form an organization and act as one body. It is based upon the personal values that each person establishes for his or her self and strives for every day. Some examples are ambition, equality, respect, and integrity. All individuals do not adhere to the same set of values; therefore personal responsibility varies from individual to individual and cannot be measured or quantified. There is no basis to determine to what degree any person or group of individuals are responsible for their actions. What may appear to be the mature and responsible thing to do for some, may not translate the same way to others facing similar circumstances. This is why we have laws. It is the duty of law to make individuals personally responsible where they otherwise might not be or are unclear to what extent they need be. For example: is it right for a man to steal bread in order to feed his children when he has exhausted ever means to acquire a loaf thru righteous efforts. Personal Responsibility says that he has an obligation to his children, to not let them go hungry. It does not however, imply that he has a responsibility not to deprive another man of his ability to feed his children. Such moral perplexities can only be resolved thru matters of law, where wisdom has determined that regardless of individual circumstances, certain acts of transgression against your fellow man are intolerable and therefore punishable.

Government cannot leave a society to be personally responsible for its self. The result would be confusion among the citizens in determining whose ideas of personal values are best suited to rule. Likewise, the people within the society cannot wholly depend on the government as an appointed body, to be personally responsible for its self. The result would ultimately be an abuse of authority by those in power against the ones that elected them to represent their interest. Hence, Bush's policy of a personally responsible (ownership) society was a flawed idea- a disastrous concept that once signed into law, left individual citizens delusional with dreams of economic freedom and property ownership beyond their means. Furthermore it left corporations, banks, and financiers who are only loyal to themselves and money unregulated. As a token of their gratitude, for this unprecedented amount of freedom, they abandoned all concepts of personal loyalty to their own country (patriotism) for greed and profit.

Let me be the first to say that Barack Obama's predecessor is not the man of limited intelligence that the media portrays him to be. In fact it takes a certain amount of genius to appear to look so aloof upon the national and international stage but yet manage to be commander and chief of the greatest nation on Earth for not one but two terms. I mean c'mon we just couldn't get enough of this guy and although I hate his policies, I still like him as a person. He's funny, and cocky, and unlike Romney, has a backbone and stands for what he believes.

Under the Bush administration, government spending went from $1,789 billion to $2,983 billion and marked the biggest increase in federal spending since LBJ. But let us not assume that Bush was just some incompetent shit kicker from Texas who couldn't govern worth a lick. But more so, let us consider that quite possibly, he's a willing participant in a much broader, calculated game designed to yield certain ideological results within his party in regards to manipulating the direction of the nation. Now more than ever the actions of modern-day Republicans contradict basic fundamental ideas that we as a nation regard as indelible rights and liberties and take for granted every day. One of these is the right to vote. During the 2012 campaign season the Republican Party tried feverously to keep voters from the polls by manipulating I.D. laws and early voting blocks. The justification for this was an effort to reduce voter fraud which historically doesn't exist. In fact a recent report by the Brennan Center for Justice concluded that **"There is no documented wave or trend of individuals voting multiple times or as someone else."** The study further concludes that although voter fraud does happen, it happens only about 0.0009% of the time, debunking the Republican's claim that they're on a mission to stop voter fraud and basically says that the whole charade was a bunch of much to do about nothing. Voter suppression is just one example of an assault on American freedom. The Republicans also notoriously attack a woman's right to choose as if they have been commissioned by god himself to be Captains of the Vaginal Guard.

The elitist seek to do away with the proclamation of *"for the people, by the people"* in an effort to seize power and bring America's workforce to its knees. Time and time again they have proven themselves to be against organized labor unions, and equal pay for equal work. Times have changed and the average American worker expects to be compensated for a full day's work at a rate comparable to the current rate of inflation. When the purchasing power of the dollar value decreases the demand for higher wages is the inevitable result. As I mentioned earlier, the absurdity of personal responsibility and economic freedom without constraint left many Americans boxed into a situation where their only means of escape was to demand higher wages at a rate much faster than the rate of economic growth for the entire country. Not to mention the rate at which the prices of goods and services were steadily increasing as they have done consistently for the last 30-40 years. The media's constant bombardment of goods and services upon the American people plays into a much larger concept of how we all define success. It entices everyone within the society to have the latest and the greatest but yet 90 percent of everything on the market is not produced here at home. In essence we wind up fueling a global economy with our hard to come by dollars and those dollars wind up in the offshore accounts of robber barons like Mitt Romney or factory workers overseas in India and China. America is no longer a formidable force amongst other industrialized nations of the world and the devaluation of the U.S. dollar on the global market is the equivalent to the beginning decline of the Roman Empire. When a country puts out more than it takes in or consumes more then it produces, it's akin to a hemophiliac on a prescribed regiment of Plavix who just can't control the bleeding.

So I ask you doctor, surely with all your years of medical practice, you have a prescription for a hurting America with more healing power than the one you've previously prescribed to me? I mean, a hefty dose of "Giv'em a taste of their own medicine" is a cynical answer and hardly a remedy for ailments and times as complex as these. But then again, perhaps it is the only answer that you and others like you have, as you fail to see the obvious answer right in front of your eyes every day. It's a simple solution to a complex problem that's been there all along or at least since the presidential election of 2008. I know what you're thinking- but no, I'm not saying that Barack Obama holds the key nor is he the answer. He's merely the manifestation of the answer to our problems. In fact the answer to the many problems that plague our nation resides within the will of the coalition of Obama voters, whose **mindset** collectively chose to overcome their doubts, prejudices, and fears in order to break tradition and boldly place upon the world stage a Black Man to represent the United States as the leader of the free world. The solution is the force behind the movement of the people that rallied behind a common purpose for good and thereby said to the status quo loud and clear- "We have overcome…"

CHAPTER 4

Less Horses and Bayonets

"Every gun that is made, every warship launched, every rocket fired, signifies in the final sense a theft from those who hunger and are not fed, those who are cold and are not clothed".
-Dwight D. Eisenhower

"There is no instance of a nation benefiting from prolonged warfare."
-Sun Tzu

The history of violence in this country dates as far back as the Boston Massacre in 1770. It was notably the first public act of violence ever recorded in American history against any group of individual citizens as it relates to the politics that would eventually shape America. Soon thereafter America would declare its independence from British rule by going to war as negotiations failed between the Parliament and members of the newly established Continental Congress. By going to war, America claimed its right to be recognized as a sovereign nation and claimed its liberty with bloodshed. Since then, a number of conflicts and strife have played key factors in the shaping of our nation's past and future. These exertions take into account the Civil War, Prohibition, and the struggle for Civil Rights. Violence has played a part in every aspect of American history including the assassination of our nation's leaders during the 1960's , to the attacks on 911 in the new millennium. Each event is evidence of America's propensity toward violence and passion for bloodshed. Some might argue that without violence we'd have no future and that violence, by some strange coincidence, is the fire in which our concepts and ideas of freedom are forged. For example the murder of Boston civilians at the time of the massacre angered the citizens so much so that it sewed seeds of resentment deep in the hearts of the colonists to the point of having no respect for British authority. For the next several years the only retaliation the colonist had were protest and public displays, and those protest culminated until they reached a tipping point at which time there was no turning back. By throwing the British Cargo into the Harbor the colonist had basically sent a message of defiance to the King of Great Britain. Parliament had no choice but to sanction young America for its act of transgression against the monarchy. And America, if it were to truly forge her own destiny, had no choice but to declare war and sacrifice her sons in the quest for freedom. Therefore, the argument can be made that America's freedom is based upon killing and the price of freedom is ultimately death. America has made this message clear to all of her enemies both domestic and foreign from day one. She is heartless in her pursuit of Democracy and global conquest, even punishing those in her own backyard if they so much as raise a hand to her. Subsequently, the enemies of America toil tirelessly day and night in an effort to uncover any weaknesses that she may possess and without any viable warrant sacrifice themselves in the name of their ideologues, zealots, and false gods in vein attempts to destroy her. Yet in spite of their persistence she continues to decimate armies and impose her will around the world.

America's enemies fail to understand that it matters not how much you are willing to become a martyr in an effort to claim a victory, in as much as it's about becoming the most technically advanced killing machine in the history of warfare. In today's world, war is first won by crippling the technological capabilities of your enemies and lastly by the use of the most technologically advanced weaponry on earth. Weaponry designed to kill with precision and accuracy. President Obama along with the leaders of our nation's military and Central Intelligence have reinforced the message of America's unyielding resolve and strength to our enemies. By using the most subtle form of warfare ever conceived in modern times, the administration has perfected the art of ambush killing to its maximum efficiency level, displaying America's strength and resolve against her enemies in the form of the MQ-1 Predator Drone. The MQ-1 has effectively changed the U.S. counter-terrorism program and the way wars will be fought in the future.

In spite of Right Wing criticism that he is a president weak on foreign policy and perhaps even a terrorist sympathizer, Obama has managed to put together an impressive kill list of Taliban generals and al- Qaeda leaders. Under President Obama's leadership drone attacks have more than tripled when compared to that of his predecessor, and has successfully lead to the execution of more than 20 top al-Qaeda officers including the head of the snake himself- Osama bin Laden. In 2009 Obama was nominated for and accepted the Nobel Peace Prize. In that same year he oversaw a military campaign that successfully executed more than 700 terrorist members of al-Qaeda and less than a year later more than doubled that number in confirmed operative kills. Al-Qaeda has been decimated and is on the run. Because of the efforts of this president, together with our nation's military and central intelligence, we are now safer than we've ever been since the war on terror began. Messages found in Osama's possession from top al-Qaeda leaders, at the time of his killing, expressed their frustration that drone strikes were taking out operatives faster than they could be replaced. There were even reports that possibly Osama's own son, Saad bin Laden had been killed in a drone strike as well. Here is some statistical data of drone strikes over the last four years:

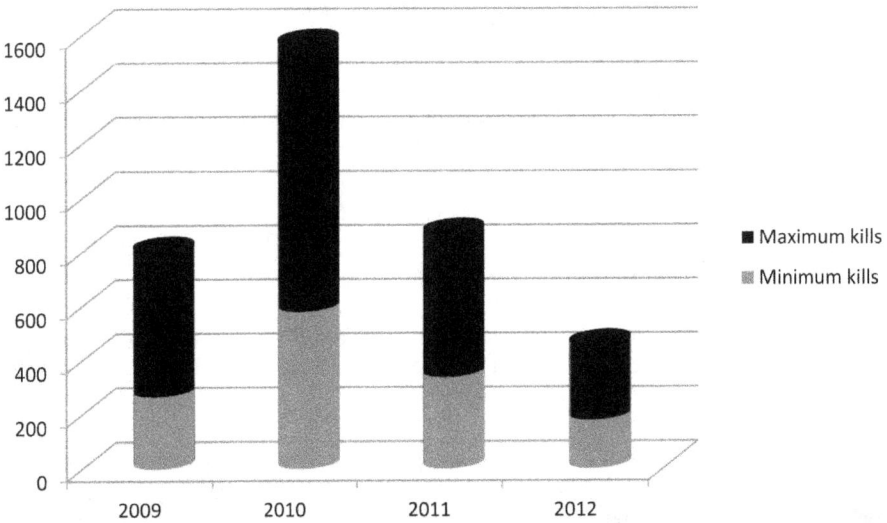

* Specific strike information can be found in the published articles of the New America Foundation study called "The Year of the Drone".

Unlike the former president Bush, Obama can boast that under his administration America is safer. Up until the recent incident in Benghazi, there had been no attacks on U.S. soil from terrorist organizations since he took office in 2009. Right Wing extremist hell bent on delegitimizing the Obama presidency, disregard Obama's success on foreign matters. They have even gone as far as to suggest that he is in bed with Muslim terrorists and is a Muslim himself. They have done everything short of suggesting that he is the Anti-Christ who will usher in the apocalypse and bring about the destruction of western civilization even as we approached the possible end of his term as president. If the president was hiding some kind of conspiratorial plan to ruin America wouldn't it seem logical that he wouldn't wait until he's up for re-election before implementing it? The absurdity of these attacks is disingenuous and outright offensive, especially to the African American community who see Barack as one of our own. During the 2012 election, polling data consistently held the presidential challenger Mitt Romney at 0% support amongst black voters. Is there any reason to wonder why? From day one, extremist, Fox news, and Right Wing talking heads have used consistent messaging to describe Barack Obama as a non-American. The hateful right, lead by such media moguls as Rush Limbaugh, Sean Hannity, Glenn Beck, Sarah Palin, (*Association of American Bullies* or A.B.A.), have stopped at nothing to express their resentment of a black man in America's White House. Franklin Graham – the son of the most ideal Christian evangelical Billy Graham, whom blacks have trusted and allowed into their homes many a Sunday morning via television airwaves, has also shown his true colors by questioning the president's faith. With no other motive than being racists and resenting the fact that an African American is in charge of the free world, he has revealed himself in the eyes of the black community as a zealot who himself is a walking contradiction of the teachings of Christ and for that matter the teachings of his own father. He along with the A. B. A. have lifted their voices together in a chorus of hatred aimed straight at the heart of America and against the very man who has sworn to protect them, and has done so by his policy of drone warfare for the past four years.

What ideologues like the members in the A. B. A. fail to take into account is the way their message is perceived by other non-white males. Essentially it says to blacks and other minorities that we hate you. Implying that gays, women, blacks, and other non-whites are taking over America and influencing the voting process. Thereby the election of Barack Obama was a fluke and an illegitimate tenure unworthy of any notability in the context and framework of our nation's history. It's a message that has its roots in segregation and Jim Crow Laws of the south which says that you are by nature inferior to us and therefore best suited for jobs that lack roles in leadership in particularly one so sovereign as the role of President. Well we've got news for them in the 21st century… the eyes & ears of the body of minority voters are neither blind nor deaf to the *Dog Whistling* attacks perpetrated by the extreme right against our shinning prince. Let me be the first to tell you white America- "Homie don't play that!" We will not stand idly by and let you destroy the legacy of this president who is a champion among our people and a jewel in the crown of our struggle to achieve equality.

One of the things that I am most baffled by is when white folks cry reverse discrimination against blacks or other minorities. Glenn Beck sat on the set of Fox news and Friends and without any respect for the office of the presidency called Barack Obama a racist who has a deep seeded hatred for white people. Sarah Palin, who is still spiteful over having her Separatist ass whooped during the 08 presidential elections and whom I could think of a slew of misogynistic idioms to refer to, had the audacity to contradict Senator John McCain during the campaign season and call Obama a terrorist. The truth of the matter is that Obama embodies a concept that real racist like Glenn Beck and Sarah Palin dread everyday which is the forward thinking and progress due by this nation to endow all men the right to achieve greatness regardless of race or creed.

In an effort to delegitimize Obama's presidency they've done everything short of calling him a nigger on public airwaves. But then again, Rick Santorum went as far to the right as possible and did that in an effort to appease republican wing nuts during the 2012 presidential primaries. I would have given him credit as a man for at least saying what he really feels, but in a cowardly display of backtracking, floundered in an attempt to make it seem as though he said anything other than the N-word when referencing the president. This is the same president, who in a speech given in front of the U.N. General Assembly said these words- "People are going to call me awful things every day and I will always defend their right to do so…"

I truly believe that Barack understands what America is about. We've all heard him say countless times that it's about fundamental ideas and core beliefs. One of which, is Rick Santorum's right to freedom of speech. But freedom of speech is not a license to use irresponsible rhetoric for the purpose of inspiring hatred. Those of us who have been called upon to speak on behalf of the public sector should have a responsibility not to incite violence amongst the nation's citizens, particularly when the demographics of the nation are changing at such drastic rates. As a nation we have become more socially divided than ever before. No longer is America simply a place of differences between blacks and whites; there are new social clashes looming on the horizon. More complex issues like sexual orientation and religion have worked their way into American social politics, differences much deeper than just your everyday issues of race. So now with so many cultural dynamics affecting U.S. policies, it is now more important than ever to be politically conscious of how hateful rhetoric is likely to offend and ostracize any number of social groups at any given time. There is always the possibility of backlash from those you offend and the manner in which that backlash presents itself can have mild to severe consequences.

If we were to look back we would see acts of terrorism by Islamic extremist on record that debut the world stage long before 911. In fact there are reported acts of terrorism associated with Islam that date back to the 11th century. In most modern times, however, there have been acts of terrorism by Islamic extremist recorded in the late 70's to early 80's. Although these attacks are not always on U.S. soil, they were in a lot of cases attacks on our allies. After 911 tensions mounted between the Middle-East and U.S. as the parties who took responsibility for the bombing began to help shape the perception to a fearful America that Islam was an evil religion. According to a report by the Pew Forum there were a reported 2.6 million Muslims living in the United States in 2010. That number is on the rise and expected to double by the year 2030 to numbers in excess of 6 million. As a knee-jerk reaction to the bombing, white Christian males in particular have a growing problem with this trend and have lashed out against members of the Arab community by profiling and branding them as terrorist. Ignorance on the part of the white Judeo-Christian male, who controlled by fear, along with the American media machine, has turned the entire world's Muslim population into the *Whipping Boy* of the new millennium and by doing so has subjected peaceful Muslim to unwarranted scrutiny and prejudice. They have used this same negative inference of Islam to describe Obama which is a further insult to members of the Muslim faith. It says to all Muslims that we (Christian America) will spare no expense toward the persecution of those will feel threaten our existence. The undertaking the U.S. government faced in breaking the spirit of the civil rights movement and pacifying blacks was one thing in regards to maintaining social hierarchy, but calming a civil unrest as a result of a culture clash between religious ideologies upon American soil would be an entirely different kind of challenge. At least with blacks, whites could find common ground in Christ centered philosophies. But when men fail to find common ground anywhere and casual dialogue turns into trivial bickering over my god is bigger than your god, which is just another way of saying I've got more guns than you, then truly the world is headed for a dangerous place.

Unfortunately the social diversity of our nation has become a political mine field for policy makers to maneuver through with the A.B.A. providing navigational direction to their followers who are also blinded by hatred. With misdirected anger, America was on the verge of persecuting all Muslims, throwing them into a cultural meat grinder regardless of orthodox until Obama's policies redefined the war on terror and focused America's resolve upon the true enemy, al-Qaeda. During the last 4-5 years, as more sensible Americans come forward, we've acquired a deeper understanding of who were fighting against, why they've waged war upon us, and where our energy must be focused in order to properly dispose of our enemies. Obama's newly defined war on terror says that Muslims are not enemies of the state and that radical extremist groups who misconstrue the teachings of Islam are. Those groups, with the assassination of their leaders, become increasingly more anxious to strike a blow for their twisted ideologies as our military becomes more and more successful in the hunt for them. It helps to have a steady governing hand behind the trigger of America's most powerful weapon, our resolve.

The presidency of Obama has a tendency to bring out very polarizing differences in how we view ourselves as Americans. Those feelings range from proud, tolerant, and patient for some to disgusted, hateful, and anxious for others. When those who feel particularly slated by Obama's tenure carry on like a bunch of whining bullies and use race baiting in order to tear down his administration, the result is an infraction against the cultural legitimacy, and religious significance of those many diverse ethnic groups who support him. They will stop at nothing and will even offend entire nations of people in their conquest to prevent what they perceive as a takeover of the American way of life, a way of life that projects the purest of blue blooded white males at the top of the social hierarchy and all others at the bottom of the food chain.

When men become led by their egos or allow their emotions to rule over them, they can no longer think objectively. A lack of objectivity leads to bad judgment and bad judgment is precisely what media monsters like Limbaugh and Palin use every day to incite violence and hatred. By doing this they fundamentally offend the many elements that make up this culture rich society we live in called America. Without fear of backlash, or regard for public safety the Association of American Bullies continue their rants against the Obama nation offending culture after culture and individual upon individual and that is Dangerous for America.

CHAPTER 5

The Run In Uncle Sam's Stocking

"For as long as the power of America's diversity is diminished by acts of discrimination and violence against people just because they are black, Hispanic, Asian, Jewish, Muslim or Gay, we still must overcome."
-Ron Kind

The movement to obtain marriage rights and benefits for gay couples began in the 1970's and became even more of a social issue in 1993 when the Hawaii Supreme court ruled on Baehr vs. Lewin. It was a lawsuit in which three same-sex couples argued that Hawaii's prohibition of same-sex marriage violated the state constitution. As the nation increasingly becomes more diversified polls show that the majority of Americans support same sex marriage in the 21st century. During an interview on May 9, 2012 hosted by ABC news anchor Robin Roberts, Barack Obama became the first sitting President to openly declare support for gay couples. Obama claimed that he had under gone an evolution on the subject. He went further to say that after being in the center of such controversial issues like overturning Don't Ask Don't Tell (DADT) and no longer defending the Defense Against Marriage Act (DOMA) he's always stood on the side of broader equality for the LGBT community. However, over the course of several years he concluded that it was important to affirm that he felt same sex couples should be able to get married. There were criticisms that Obama was merely reacting to comments made by Vice-President Joe Biden where he was the first member within the president's cabinet to signal support for gay marriage during an interview on Sunday's Meet the Press. Because gay marriage is such a sensitive issue and due to a lack of knowing how to properly respond to the Presidents declaration, hard Right Wingers like Fox News journalist, Michael Goodwin hurried to criticize Obama for not holding a press conference where reporters, like himself, could ask more probing questions about his decision to make the announcement. He went further to say that Roberts was chosen to break the story because she was black, female, and possibly lesbian. Goodwin went even further implying that ABC had been played by the administration in order to get the story out. Besides Goodwin's nonsensical comments, there were further assertions by the Right that the president was using the gay marriage issue to score political points on the eve of the election season— Imagine that!

The GOP has always been outspoken on their disdain for gay lifestyles and homosexuality, adamantly holding on to the position that marriage is between one man and one woman. They use the bible as the foundation for their opposition against gays and interpret certain scriptures as speaking directly on the subject of homosexuality. What I find interesting as a writer is the same group of people who want less government and oppose bureaucrats in Washington telling them what to do are the same hypocrites willing to impose their beliefs upon others. None the less, the bible has conveniently become the basis for condemning homosexuality with the passage of Sodom and Gomorrah at the cornerstone of the debate. Christians argue that the men of Sodom wished to rape the Angels sent to retrieve Lot, implying of course that the angels were of male gender. The name Sodom as become the basis of the word sodomy which is a popular synonym for anal sex. Noted author Rev. Candace Chellew-Hodge argued that the six or so passages in the bible often used as fuse against homosexuality are in fact referencing "abusive sex". She goes as far as to maintain that there were no condemnations for gay couples in the bible and that Jesus was silent on the matter. Yet despite Jesus being silent on the matter Republican's remain outspoken.

As a minority group, same sex marriage couples continue to fight for basic rights and equalities that are afforded to every other American household, however the Defense of Marriage Act (DOMA) keeps their struggle at the state level as opposed to being litigated in the Federal courts. DOMA was enacted in 1996 as a reaction to same sex arguments moving up the courts in the 80's and 90's. DOMA essentially prevents the Federal Government from recognizing same sex marriage and forces the individual states to deal with these issues. It implicitly states that marriage is the union of one man and one woman. Currently only 8 states recognize same sex marriage:

- Iowa
- Massachusetts
- New Hampshire
- Vermont
- New York
- Connecticut
- Maryland
- Rhode Island

Let it be noted that there are no Southern states within this group of progressives as the conservative South clings to traditional marriage values denying same sex couples benefits that traditional couples take advantage of every day. For instance, under Federal law married couples are entitled to:

- Social Security Benefits
- Veteran Benefits
- Medicaid
- Hospital Visitation
- Pensions

However, many aspects of marriage law are determined at the state level. DOMA is currently under challenge within the federal court system as Judge Joseph Tauro of the District Court of Massachusetts deemed that under the 10th amendment, denial of federal rights and benefits was unconstitutional to those lawfully married in Massachusetts.

Another pressing issue with homosexuality in the 21st century is the issue of gays in the military. Most of the military forces of the world have removed policies prohibiting non heterosexual individuals from serving. I was surprised to see that among those nations were: the U.N. Security Council, The Republic of China, Australia, Israel, Argentina, France, Russia, and all NATO members except Turkey. If a man is to be truly noted for championing the issues of our time, and those times indicate an overwhelming affinity by the people to recognize a dynamic cultural shift in ideology, like accepting same sex couples as a normal part of society, then Obama should be credited with successfully ending the policy of Don't Ask Don't Tell against gays in the U.S. military during his tenure as President of the United States.

Besides the usual arguments of immorality against gays, Conservatives argue that the presence of gays serving openly within the military poses risk to morale and threatens the cohesion of the units that the military deems essential.

There are an estimated 4 million (about 1.7% of the population) reported gays in the United States according to an article published by the Huffington Post. Gary Gates, a demographer at the Williams Institute on Sexual Orientation Law and Public Policy at the University of California says that number may be less as previous studies often lump those who openly say they are gay with those who reportedly sometimes engage in homosexual acts, implying that there are emphatic differences between those who use the term to describe themselves vs. sexual behavior or attraction. In the same token around another 1.8 % (just over 4 million) claim they are openly bisexual. Now here's the kicker, Gates further estimated that another 19 million or 8.2% of the adult population have had sex with a partner of the same gender and that there is an estimated 700,000 transgender adults amongst the population. WHEW! That's a lot of VOTES…The Republican Party emphatically approved a party platform during the 2012 RNC Convention that would ban all abortions and gay marriages totally disregarding the fact that our Nation's Demographic makeup is changing, perhaps even downplaying the fact that a significant portion of their own party's constituents fall into one of the many categories of sexual orientation mentioned within this paragraph. The LGBT community is a permanent and growing part of the American electorate and the GOP would be wise to find ways to include them as part of their dwindling base as opposed to alienating them on the floor of the house, pulpits of the church, and the national media.

A joint study conducted by the University of Rochester, University of Essex, and University of California found that homophobia is more pronounced in individuals with an acknowledged attraction to the same sex who most likely grew up with imperious parents who looked down on such desires. These are the ones who are quick to chastise others for being different, yet under the surface have so much in common with those they look down their nose at.

In November 2006, conservative evangelical pastor Ted Haggard fell under accusations of having a homosexual relationship with male escort and masseur Mike Jones. Jones alleged that Haggard paid him for sex for three years and that haggard had also purchased and used Crystal Meth on occasion. Haggard ranted in the pulpit for years against homosexuality while maintaining a prominent position as leader of the National Association of Evangelicals and founder of the New Life Church of Colorado. He was a firm supporter of George W. Bush and was reported to talk to Bush or a member of his staff every Monday. He was strongly credited with rallying many evangelicals behind Bush and in 2005 became one of Time Life's top 25 evangelicals in America. Nearly 5 years after the scandal broke Haggard was quoted in G.Q. Magazine as saying… "If I were 21 in this society, I would identify myself as a bisexual."

Another example of those who perpetuate the hypocrisy against the LGBT community is Former U.S. Senator Larry Craig who is also a member of the Republican

Party and a lifelong member of the National Rifle Association. In August of 2007, a Capitol Hill newspaper revealed that Craig had been arrested for lewd conduct in a public restroom at St Paul International Airport where he allegedly solicited an undercover officer for sex. Despite denying the accusations against him he eventually pleads guilty to a misdemeanor charge of disorderly conduct by signing a petition that conveyed the following: "I now make no claim that I am innocent of the charge to which I am entering a plea of guilty." Just months before his arrest ,Craig led the charge against Barney Frank for his participation in a gay prostitution scandal and openly criticized President Bill Clinton for his inappropriate conduct during the Monica Lewinsky ordeal.

Whether or not Larry Craig likes to have sex in public restrooms, or Haggard likes getting high while getting his freak on with his male masseuse before Sunday morning service should not be our concern. What should concern us is the dishonest nature of these men who claim to be ordained by god or are chosen through the voting process to represent the public sector. These masters of deception falsely represent who they really are and deceive the public into appointing them to be stewards over the issues that affect the voters' lives the most. These men are the worst kind of hypocrites who lead the charge against the gay and lesbian community while secretly indulging in the very lifestyle they criticize others for.

If every person is responsible for his or her own deeds when standing in front of the All Mighty come judgment day, what business is it of Conservative extremist to scrutinize the lifestyle of those who choose to love members of the same sex? Let each man answer for himself when he is called to judgment, the reality is that it can be no other way, I can't account for the things that John Doe has done any more then he can account for the things I've done. Can you imagine the Lord asking Ted Haggard on judgment day– "Why has thou not rid the earth of all the same sex sinners?" Now imagine Haggard's response- "Because Lord, I couldn't control my own desires for men much less the desires of others..." Remember that concept we discussed back in chapter 3 about personal responsibility? Here is a perfect example of how one man's values can hardly be the archetype for the values of all other men. Haggard is one of a long line of evangelical hypocrites caught up homosexual scandals dating as far back as the 1970's. Lonnie Frisbee, although a confessed homosexual, was forced to leave the church after allegations of Frisbee's relationship with a young boy surfaced in an Orange County Weekly article. The church managed to keep truths about Frisbee's lifestyle from the congregation throughout his career but was forced to acknowledge it when the allegations surfaced in the paper. Some of the more recent preacher scandals involving homosexuality are George Allen Rekers, Eddie Long, and Albert Odulele. All of whom preached against homosexuality yet carried on affairs with men behind closed doors.

Perhaps not as quite disgusting as a hypocrite preacher but just as distasteful, is a hypocritical member of public office. It turns out Larry Craig isn't alone in the category of hypocritical office holders. Mark Foley (U.S. Congressman) known for pushing anti-gay policies, was forced to resign after allegation surfaced that he had sent sexually explicit emails and instant messages to several young male house staffers. Bob Allen who is currently serving as a Florida State representative was arrested after offering to perform oral sex on a male officer in a public park restroom in exchange for $20. Allen maintains his innocence stating the only reason why he offered to perform the fellatio deed was because he felt intimidated by the big black muscular man in the restroom. Of these I find the actions of this next wanker the most appalling. James "Jim" West (Mayor of Spokane Washington) who is a known anti-gay Republican came under scrutiny after allegation surfaced that he sexually molested members of his Boy-Scout troop twenty years before taking public office. He also came under fire when his hometown newspaper (Spokane Review) conducted a sting operation after an unknown source alleged that the Identity of the man behind user name Cobra82 on a gay.com website was West. The newspaper created a false user name (Motobrock) and began engaging Cobra82 on the site. Motobrock then arranged to meet with Cobra82 on a golf field where newspaper officials verified that Cobra82 was in fact James West thus proving his level of hypocrisy among the highest of hypocrites.

If these individuals would just be themselves and take on a little *personal responsibility*, the American public would have no problem with them. If your gay then BE GAY, polls show the majority of Americans are on your side, but to run around self righteously promoting anti-gay policies and in other instances bashing gays while you secretly carry on affairs with members of the same sex and even prey on children in some cases is the height of hypocrisy.

Obama's stance on gay rights is one that members of the Right Wing dread, largely because it falls in line with libertarian values. It shows empathy for members of the gay community and makes them more partial to Democratic Party affiliation. In the past Republicans have taken such a strong stance against gay marriage and homosexuality that it becomes increasingly difficult to persuade the base of their party to view same sex issues more open mindedly. This is what happens when political leaders use their influence to shape opinions instead of simply providing the necessary information and letting the people form conscious decisions for themselves. The constituents become brainwashed and nearly impossible to un-train as the world continues to evolve around them. Their views become obsolete and backward thinking becomes the new normalcy.

There are so many different elements within the American culture that it's hard not to praise one without offending the other. But what's important for us all to remember is that our pledge to the allegiance of this country includes- "One nation, under God, indivisible, with liberty and justice for all." When so many of our leaders are willing to persecute others for not loving the same way they do or choosing a lifestyle outside the traditional confines of marriage and equality, they have gone against the very pledge that they've indoctrinated us all to believe in since our first day of school. What makes their ideology so much more appropriate than others who cling to the right to love freely? When men place themselves on moral pedestals and look down upon their brothers and sisters in resentment because they are different, they not only toss aside the values that make this country great but they keep American's divided and at odds with one another and that's *Dangerous for America.*

CHAPTER 6

Foot-N-Mouth Disease

"I voted Republican this year; the Democrats left a bad taste in my mouth."
-Monica Lewinsky

It's the morning after the re-election of Obama and coincidentally trash day in my neighborhood. I found it delightfully funny to see once proud Right Wing supporters remove Romney/Ryan signs from their yards and toss them on the curb along side of endless garbage cans all over my community. I could tell their level of frustration with the election results by the manner in which they disposed of each sign. Some laid there signs gingerly against their rubber cans while others ripped their signs and shamefully stuffed them down into their containers as far as they could as if to leave no evidence of their support. Up until the day of the election I entertained myself by counting the number of Romney signs vs. Obama signs while driving around my subdivision. Although I knew it was foolish notion, a certain part of me felt like counting the signs would reveal some insight into the outcome of the election. I started writing on this subject shortly after the initial primary season where Republican nominees went through a series of front runners and ultimately wound up with Mitt Romney as the nominee. I watched Mitt change from a moderate conservative Governor of Massachusetts, to in his own words a "Severe Conservative" who chose to consciously flip-flop on issue after issue and run the most dishonest campaign in the history of American politics.

In a move that reinforced the legitimacy of his presidency, Barack Obama handed Republican challenger Mitt Romney a stunning defeat during the 2012 election that left hardcore conservatives and Obama haters across the country in utter disbelief. Republicans, for the last four years, convinced themselves that the election of the first African American President was a fluke, an anomaly unworthy of recognition in the pages of American history. The reality that America is a nation in the midst of enormous change had finally set in and the height of misinformation by the Right Wing media machine, like the wheels of a runaway freight train, had abruptly come to a screeching halt. When it was all said and done Obama had mopped the floor with his opponent winning both the popular vote and electoral vote by overwhelming numbers. Not only did the electoral map, for the most part remain unchanged, but Obama also managed to expand his support in several key battleground states. The old guard in the form of the Southern Coalition did manage to show their support for the Republican challenger, but in the end it just wasn't enough. Obama's victory is all the more proof that the old America is out and the changing of the guard was permanently signified by America's refusal to move backwards and re-live antiquated laws and ways of thinking. The old guard is stubborn and above all else racist, yet ironically it is those Southern states that are most in need of education reform and social services and other federally funded programs which they refuse to take advantage of because of their biases.

Since Romney's defeat, the A.B.A have been in rare form attributing Obama's success to everything from Hurricane Sandy stopping Romney's momentum to left wing efforts to suppress the conservative vote. I've even heard one pundit say that Candy Crowley was to blame for backing the President during the 2nd debate over whether or not he identified the Benghazi incident as a terrorist attack. Some pundits have gone as far as to say that the white man is the new minority in America. Others have said that the GOP simply doesn't do enough to keep up with the changing face of American culture. But the one that tickles me the most is the excuse given by the actual failed contender himself,

Mitt Romney- "Obama gave out gifts to African Americans, Hispanics, and young people in the form of welfare, citizenship, and contraceptives." –he replied in an interview on Fox News shortly after the election. Here we have Romney proving once and for all that all the money in the world couldn't buy him a clue if he were Conan Doyle himself. The Romney Campaign relied heavily on polling data and was confident they had closed the gap on Obama after a successful first debate performance. However, no amount of polling data could predict the enthusiasm of individuals who aren't driven to the polls by any party affiliation, or are not persuaded by the daily rants of media pundits one way or another. It also helps to see their president on the nightly news displaying basic human emotions as he deals with crisis after crisis; they too share a similar reaction as they realize how much those crisis impact their own lives.

The re-election of Obama also signifies a great change in the value system of America. It says that we are no longer a nation of slavers and enslaved people, that we're not just a nation of servants to the super rich. We are independent and free to make our own decisions and will do so by exercising our right to vote in a conscious manner and choose our leaders appropriately, not by having our leaders dictated to us or determined by the highest bidder.

Based upon the election results Republicans must admit that it was a pretty naïve notion to believe Romney (someone whom they never really liked in the first place) could defeat an incumbent president with a likability rating as high as Obama has maintained throughout his tenure. People like Obama and feel a kindred connection to him. He embodies the essence of the underdog and in many ways is a lot like Seamus, who Mitt Romney strapped to the roof of his car for 12 hours. White folks are always trying to take black folks for a ride... For instance, they took us for a ride when they promised us equal housing but failed to inform us that racially restrictive covenants in real estate were unenforceable in court. This put blacks returning home from World War II at a considerable disadvantage as they were consistently met with patterns of segregation and discrimination regardless of the act and serving their country. Or how about ending school segregation but then making all the best text books available to schools in predominately white communities? Whether by accident or intention, America's wealthiest citizens alienate the poorest among us every day and it doesn't help the situation, what so ever, when a presidential candidate for office makes reference to 47% of Americans as tax dodgers who are predisposed to vote Democratic. It's funny how I never heard this mentioned as one of the possible reasons for Mitt Romney's defeat by conservatives pundits. The truth of the matter is that during the campaign season Republicans, as a whole, stuck their foot in their mouths on a litany of issues that quite possibly affected their chances of re-taking the White House. In fact the 2012 election might go down in history as the election of the most self inflicted wounds by any one party.

The old Republican guard with its antiquated ways of thinking danced on the razors edge when tackling issues of women's health care. One woman close to me said, and I quote- "If a woman doesn't want to have a baby she shouldn't have to have a baby;

but if she does decide to have a baby, then she doesn't want a president that will take away her access to healthcare that will ensure the quality of life for her baby." Several times throughout the election process the issues of contraception and abortion became the main subject of our national conversation. Each time it appeared to be a knee jerk reaction to something the president's administration had proposed or some insanely ridiculous public statement made by a member of the Republican Party. When the administration made it mandatory for any institution receiving federal funding to provide insurance coverage for contraception to its employees, the Catholic Church and Conservatives went ballistic. They argued that of course the federal government had overstepped its boundaries and infringed upon the sovereignty of separation between church and state. The problem was that although the Catholic Church doesn't receive federal subsidies, many of the hospital and other faith based institution that they oversee do. This controversy was the first to bring the issue of contraception to the forefront during the 2012 election. It gave Big Heads like Newt Gingrich and Rush Limbaugh a platform at which they could hammer away at the president for his position on the matter although ironically more than 80% of Catholic women as well as men use some form of contraception or another against the ordinance of the Catholic Church. Gingrich blasted the president calling Obama an extremist that supported infanticide. Even Romney spoke out against the administration saying-   "I don't think we've seen in the history of this country the kind of attack on religious freedom we've seen in Barack Obama most recently requiring the Catholic Church to provide for its employees and its various enterprises health care insurance that would include birth control, sterilization and the morning after pill," he said. "He tried to retreat from that, but he retreated in a way that was not appropriate, because these insurance companies have to provide these same things, and now the Catholic Church will have to pay for them." The mandate had stirred up quite a controversy and for a minute it seemed as though the Republican argument was gaining traction until a remarkable young woman entered the national spotlight.

Sandra Fluke, Georgetown University Law graduate and women's rights advocate first gained national recognition when, in a bigoted move, the House Republicans refused to allow her to testify to the House Oversight Committee on the importance of requiring insurance plans to cover birth control. She later spoke exclusively to Democratic members of the house who welcomed her testimony as open minded members of any progressive society with values should. After hearing of Fluke's remarks to the Democratic Committee, the biggest, baddest, member of the Association of American Bullies (Rush Limbaugh) mocked and scoffed at the young attorney during his radio talk-show program making inflammatory accusations about her sexuality while calling her a slut and prostitute. It didn't stop there; Limbaugh went on a tirade for 3 days against Fluke in which he repeatedly used misogynistic terms to describe the young lady whom he had never even met.

We all, as a nation witnessed the compassion of Barack Obama to stand up for young women when, like a father, he came out and condemned Limbaugh's phallicist attack against the young Sandra Fluke and shielded her from the verbal assaults of the Nation's top bully. We also witnessed the non- caring, self absorbency of Mitt Romney, who had so much to say about the issue of contraception early on but chose to remain pretty much silent when one of *America's Daughters* was so viciously attacked by a member of his own political party. Romney, unlike a father of any kind, refused to condemn Limbaugh merely stating - "Well those weren't the words I would have used..." I like many other Americans failed to see a leader in Mitt Romney at that particular moment and this, as well as a litany of other examples, became huge moments of missed opportunities for the contingent next president to prove his readiness for such a high calling.

Republican missteps on this issue alone gave Obama a huge edge with women voters throughout the remaining months of the campaign but it wasn't enough to hold their misogynistic rhetoric at bay. Whether it was Richard Mourdock's perception of God's intention to impregnate victims of rape or Todd Aiken's definition of *Legitimate Rape*, the G.O.P. failed to reassure women during the 2012 campaign that they were indeed competent to handle women's issues from a 21st Century perspective as opposed to ending years of progress by the feminist movement with age old dogmatic positions on what women's roles are in society.

Romney's overseas trip during the 2012 election will probably go down as one of the worst appearances by a presidential candidate on the world stage ever. I was embarrassed as an American when watching media coverage of Mitt's Follies in between 2012 Olympic coverage. I remember asking myself, how on earth we could even consider electing such an imbecile to represent us; I had to remind myself that opposition to Obama's re-election had little to do with Romney's ability to appear presidential and everything to do with Obama's ability to be presidential. As disappointed as I was in Romney's overseas performance I remained hopeful that he would end his trip on a better note. I am by no means a Romney hater, as I mentioned earlier, I watched him go from the moderate Republican Governor of Massachusetts that applied sensible policies and approved legislation that reformed health care, to (in his own words) an extremely conservative Governor that would bend over as far right as the extremist Republican party would have him to. I had hoped for my American brother to represent us appropriately and recover from his fumble of insulting the English and their readiness for the Olympic Games but unfortunately Romney managed to say something stupid at each of his scheduled stops along the way. Some believe that Romney's gaffe in London was not so much a mix up of words as it was a testament to his personal character. I happen to believe that his Praise of Israel's wealth and technological prowess, that ended up as an insult to the Palestinians, was in fact a true testament of his character as similarly he wound up making the same kind of statement against 47% of Americans during a fund raiser here at home. Romney tried to back track later on by saying that he didn't speak about the Palestinian culture what so ever but Fred Kaplan from Slate news said it best. "If someone says whites are better off than blacks because of culture, they are very clearly talking about black culture as well as white culture." Without sounding cliché, it would seem that the only thing wealthy people respect is other wealthy people with more money. Just as Romney ostracized the Palestinians for their lack of wealth and prowess he ostracized millions of Americans for their lack of ability to earn enough income to pay taxes and thus their lack of wealth. Romney's 47% gaffe was not so much a game changer as countless forced errors had already contributed to that, more so it was the final nail in his political coffin that was custom fitted to Romney's precise specifications as post election results would ultimately reward him with 47% of the electorate when it was all said and done.

Romney was not the first wealthy candidate to ever run for the office of president. There were several others. However much of politics is a stagecraft and unlike his predecessor Ronald Reagan, he lacked the ability to hand the audience (voters) a believable performance worthy of any recognition beyond that of slapstick. Being a man of great wealth, a lot of which was handed down to him from wealthy parents, it was difficult for Romney to identify with problems that everyday Americans were facing. He couldn't do the simplest of things like sit with folks from the town's local bakery without insulting their cookies or make casual jokes about being unemployed without insulting their intelligence.

As a young man I discovered that I bonded and shared the interest of those I had the most in common with. There were a significant number of us in my neighborhood and we didn't take to kindly of outsiders who we didn't know or weren't like us. As I got older I realized that my responsibilities had changed and subsequently I found myself making new friends and shaking off old allegiances that didn't share my new values. These days I find myself most interested in looking out for my family and those associates I have the most in common with. I believe it is basic human nature to adopt these kinds of principal interests in life and therefore not difficult at all, once you get to know a person, to see where their loyalties lie. Romney's failure was not his apparent lack of concern for poor people; it was an inability to relate and express commonality with everyday struggling middle class Americans. For instance, why else would he tell an audience full of students receiving federal aid in order to attend school at Otterbein University, to barrow money from their parents in order to start a business? According to the National Center for Education Statistics the school has an enrollment of just over 3,000 students, 87% of which are white, for any given year. Out of that number of enrollees- 100% of them receive some form of financial assistance, 99% of which are receiving institutional aid of $14,022 on average. It was insensitive to say the least but even beyond that, outrageous for a man born with a silver spoon in his mouth to suggest to a room full of financial aid recipients to barrow 10's of thousands of dollars from their parents in order to start a business. The president suggested during the campaign that Romney suffers from some kind of Amnesia; perhaps this is true because it's like he forgets with whom he is speaking to sometimes. With loyalty ties to the wealthiest among us, his perception of the American way of life is starkly different from the realities that most struggling Americans face every day. He even admitted in his speech the stature of those in his friendship circle by using Jimmy John as an example. Jimmy John is rich; his father, whom he borrowed money from to start his business, Jim Liautaud is rich and made millions as the founder of Capsonic Group, a manufacturer of composite plastics and inserts which he supplies to GM and Ford. The Jimmy Johns franchise flourished under the Obama administration establishing over 1200 location in 40 states and opened approximately 200 units per year for the last 3 years. In truth, the Liautaud family has done well and should be thanking the president for saving the auto industry, which a great deal of their family success is directly connected to. But instead, the founder of Jimmy Johns went on fox news and adamantly expressed his support for Mitt Romney and publicly criticized Obama Care in a heedless example of non-appreciation and contempt.

The cumulative, mindset of the entire Republican Party was on stage during the 2012 campaign season where they revealed themselves as far right extremist on a host of issues. Yes, Mitt Romney had an abundance of help from his colleagues in the G.O.P. with looking like the party most out of touch with practical America. We don't exist independent of one another and we understand that it takes each of us doing our individual parts to make this country work on a much broader scale. Romney's notion of pulling yourself up by your own boot straps or campaign rhetoric that says "You didn't build that!" didn't go over well with the American people and met a dead end on election day. The Republican primary season was not so much a series of debates as it was a cacophony of sexist, racist, angry rhetoric aimed particularly at the heart of the progressive movement in this country symbolized by the election of Obama. Their resounding theme became *"Taking America Back"*, but back from whom and back to what?

Here is a list of *out of this world* gaffes by the Republican Party during the 2012 Election:

Rick Santorum- *The Moralist*
- $\frac{35}{17}$ During an interview in a room full of white voters said in reference to welfare- "I don't want to make black people's lives better by giving them someone else's money."
- $\frac{35}{17}$ Had a Freudian slip of the tongue and called Obama an Anti war, government, Nigger
- $\frac{35}{17}$ "I understand why Obama wants to send every kid to college, because of their indoctrination mills absolutely," Said that college indoctrinates kids into secular world views.

Newt Gringrich- *The Braniac*
- $\frac{35}{17}$ Told a crowd of voters while campaigning in Florida "By the end of my second term we will have the first permanent base on the moon and it will be American."
- $\frac{35}{17}$ "It's tragic what we do in the poorest neighborhoods, entrapping children in…child laws, which are truly stupid. Most of these schools ought to get rid of unionized janitors, have one master janitor and pay local students to take care of the schools" The kids would actually do work, they would have cash, they would have pride in the schools, they'd begin the process of rising.
- $\frac{35}{17}$ "Black Americans should demand jobs, not food stamps…"

Ron Paul- *The Outlier*

$\frac{35}{17}$ The government itself runs a fraud much bigger than Madoff's. Our social Security system is the very definition of a Ponzi, or pyramid scheme. If the government truly had an interest in protecting peoples savings, they would allow people to opt of Social security altogether. We would cut wasteful spending such as our overseas empire, to honor current obligations to seniors, and eventually phase the program out. Instead as with Enron and Sarbanes Oxley, I expect new, unrelated legislation to be proposed that further damages freedom in the name of protecting us."

$\frac{35}{17}$ It's time to treat all drugs the way we treat alcohol and cigarettes, substances that kill millions more than drugs do. The drug war allows drug lords to make a lot more money than legalized drugs ever would."

Mitt Romney- *The Aristocrat*

$\frac{35}{17}$ During a time of economic uncertainty and in spite being known for his lack of sensitivity to the poor told an audience of a 1,000 business men "my wife, Ann drives a couple of Cadillac's…"

$\frac{35}{17}$ "I'm not concerned about the very poor…we have a safety net there."

$\frac{35}{17}$ "There are 47 percent of the people who will vote for the president no matter what. All right, there are 47 percent who are with him, who are dependent upon government, who believe that they are victims, who believe the government has a responsibility to care for them, who believe that they are entitled to health care, to food, to housing, to you-name-it -- that that's an entitlement. And the government should give it to them. And they will vote for this president no matter what. ... These are people who pay no income tax. ... My job is not to worry about those people. I'll never convince them they should take personal responsibility and care for their lives."

Todd Aiken- *The Boob*

$\frac{35}{17}$ "…If it's a legitimate rape, the female body has ways to shut that whole thing down."

Richard Mourdock- *The Ejaculate Conceptionist*

$\frac{35}{17}$ Said during a debate that "even when life begins in that horrible situation of rape- that is something that God intended to happen."

I happen to like Governor Rick Perry so I'm not going to call him out for forgetting which three agencies of government he would so passionately do away with during the Republican debate, nor for going hunting at Nigger Head Ranch. Heck, I've often wondered what a Nigger Head Euro sticker might look like on the back of my truck window alongside my current Hilton Head Euro, because of course, any destination resort with a fancy name like that ought to be open to the American public. I won't even throw him under the bus for his Anti-Gay media endorsement that got him banned from YouTube, which I think was a first of its kind. But I will say that there were some other candidate bums in 2012 primaries that aren't even worth mentioning within the context of good literature and useful information.

So Chris Christie can sleep at night knowing in full confidence that his bromance with Obama during the Hurricane Sandy disaster had very little if not nothing to do with the results of the election. If I were Christie I'd remind Republicans of Romney's suicidal jump off the political cliff during the second debate when he challenged the President on the Benghazi issue and got served. My family and I, till this day, love to sit around the dinner table and mock the event where Obama told Romney in plain English- "Proceed Governor..." It was like watching Wile E. Coyote trying to catch the Road Runner with one of those mail order ACME traps that never work.

In order to defeat Obama the G.O.P. were willing to entertain a wide range of extremist, philanderers, and nit-wits to run against him and ultimately settled for the later of the three. In retrospect, any one of the G.O.P. candidates could have run against the incumbent and stood a chance at winning as is the very nature of our politics. Who knows for sure if the real Mitt Romney would have eventually come forward to assume the role he so desperately sought after had he been handed a victory? All we know is that the candidate that showed up for several months during the debates was not a person that the American people or even his own party could support 100% and the idea that he or anyone of the other G.O.P. candidates could have been our next sitting president of the United States is a scary thought. However, in desperation the G.O.P. rallied behind Mitt Romney, not with hopes of making him the next President but with hopes of removing the first black president from the White House. It didn't matter to them whether or not their candidate was qualified; instead Republican voters went to the polls lead by their emotions and void of any rational thinking to cast their ballots and that is *Dangerous for America.*

CHAPTER 7

The Gift of Immense Power

"The day I'm inaugurated, this country looks at itself differently and the world looks at America differently. If you believe that we've got to heal America and we've got to repair our standing in the world, then I think my supporters believe that I am a messenger who can deliver that message around the world in a way that no other candidate can do."
-Barack Obama

What greater gift could a nation offer its people than real leadership they can be proud of? There's no finer example than one that signifies to the rest of the world a county's strength, union, and innovative drive- but most importantly basic regard for the principles of human life and dignity. The kind of leadership that shines like a beacon for other nations to look upon in adoration and perhaps even envy with hopes that their leaders, will too one day, lead them into a world of endless possibilities and freedom to be as innovative as their hearts desire. Such is the vision of the American way of life to countless people all over the world. To many, America is a place where dreams come true. Where people have the right to express an opinion without being punished and are able to choose who their representatives are without having them dictated to. It's a place where people can come and go as they please and feel safe in their beds a night. Yes, to many she is the 8th wonder of the world. And it's accomplishments like that of Barack Obama that reinforce these perceptions of America to citizens of other nations.

Obama's inauguration in 2009 brought with it tremendous energy from around the world as people began to latch on to new ideas of hope and independence, civility and peace. Obama was like a breath of fresh air to an otherwise dying planet riddled with wars and discourse. During the Bush Era, America had worn out her welcome among many nations and became known as an importunate bully during U.N. negotiations and peace talks. The Iraq war had consequently left America hugely unpopular amongst other nations and citizens the world over began turning away from us as our *Light* grew hopelessly dim.

We needed someone to re-ignite the fire from within us as a country, symbolized by the torch Lady Liberty holds within her hand. We could not afford to have our flame diminished by a legacy of bad foreign policy or disregard for human life. The torch of liberty must remain lit as an example to other nations. There's something unique about the element of fire. Like the human body it needs oxygen in order to breathe. It expels carbon dioxide in the form of waste just as we do. It can be helpful or equally harmful depending on its usage and without it we cannot exists. America is the light of the world and the fire by which all other nations exist. If we choose leaders who, for whatever reason, lack or aren't getting an appropriate amount of oxygen to their brain, then intelligent decisions will not be made in regards to diplomacy and our light will be extinguished. Our contributions to the world will be harmful to society and as a result nothing useful will come from us as a nation under their governance. Thus the world will have to look elsewhere for leadership. So we must choose leaders more prudently in upcoming elections. We must not give into our emotions when casting our vote at the polls and we most certainly cannot afford to allow any member of the voter electorate to feel alienated because of race or ethnicity. We have to elect leaders who are mindful of the impact that our decisions make around the world. Who understand the speed at which information travels and the potential harm that one bad media image can do to a nation otherwise trying to clean up its act.

I was speaking to my spouse one morning trying to update her on the progress of this book. I told her that I was off to a good start on chapter 7 and that within it, I wanted to describe how the re-election of Obama opens up a world of possibilities as far as candidate choices for Democrats in 2016. Obama's re-election symbolizes many different things but perhaps the most significant is the fact that young people are now, more than ever, actively involved in the voting process and with choosing how they want to be represented. As a voting group, they have fundamentally changed the politics of America and conversations around the dinner table putting our nation on track for a total transformation. Republicans know that if this trend continues, as it has for the past two election cycles, the impact could forever change the way we look at politics in this country and could perhaps even mean the demise of their party if they are unable to adopt new policies. Obama's election in 2008 meant that the proverbial "Glass Ceiling" in America had finally been broken. His re-election in 2012 equally meant that it was not by accident and Republicans are left to clean up the mess. Now more than ever the possibilities are endless and we could definitely be looking at other non-traditional front-runners in 2016. "It's time to take these possibilities seriously…" is what the *Old Guard* is saying to itself in these early post election days. Little do they realize that the current generation of young voters have already considered the outcomes and by re-electing Obama have pre-set the stage for a Hillary Rodham Clinton victory in 2016. This time it will be different. America is ready for new leadership and a Hillary Rodham Clinton candidacy would represent a different kind of run for president by a woman in politics. Many predict that she would be uncontested by even the most qualified of white men (traditional candidates) currently within the field. Already we've seen Republicans and the Right Wing media machine attack Hillary over Benghazi in a pre-emptive attempt to tarnish her reputation for 2016 and they're just getting started. We witnessed the frivolous attack by the Right Wing on Susan Rice immediately following the president's re-election over this same issue. Those of us in the black community knew what that was all about. The Old Guard was not going to allow two prominent black figureheads to be the face of America on both the domestic front and abroad so long as they could help it. As a country we owe it to ourselves to push beyond the boundaries of normal expectations and fulfill a lifelong vision in this country of true equality for all. Until then, we are merely playing a game that doesn't end with any real winners.

It takes a visionary to transform a nation like Lincoln did during the mid 1800's. Lincoln had the foresight to realize that every man could contribute to the greatness of our Nation whether he is black or white. In his heart he knew that slavery was wrong and expressed resentment of the institution both candidly and openly as often as he could. Let's be clear, not all of our elected presidents have been visionaries. In order to be a visionary you have to display certain attributes like appearing to be a little fanciful, dreamlike, or extravagant. You have to latch onto an idea that things could be a certain way, provided that the proper frame work has been laid in order for it to come to fruition, and otherwise break from the status quo. Often times we gauge the greatness of an individual on his or her ability to sell their vision to others, to make others realize the value in what they're proposing and subsequently getting us all to move in that direction. So it takes a certain amount of gumption in order to make one's vision a reality for all. Other's have tried and soon realized that it's easier to move mountains than break traditional customs like having all white males at the apex of American politics. Shirley Chisholm had the vision in 1972. Even though the odds of her becoming president were a million to one, with different goals in mind for those days and those times, her legacy was a campaign of *consciousness*. Hillary, should she choose to run, will be a campaign of *cognizance*. An acknowledgment to the powers that be- "We have overcome…we will no longer be bound by the nature of yesterday's politics where corruption, greed, and racial biases set the tone for the type conversations we have in America." A nation of free thinkers has emerged from the ashes of 911 and the bloodshed of Sandy Hook Elementary. We want to feel secure without feeling oppressed; we want to raise our children without guns in their classrooms and we want our political process to be fair and not bought and paid for by Super Pac loyalists.

CHAPTER 8

White Folks Be Trip'n

"I don't believe in fate or destiny. I believe in various degrees of hatred, paranoia, and abandonment. However much of that gets heaped upon you doesn't matter – it's only how much you can take and what it does to you."
-Howard Rollins

I can remember growing up thinking that the Boogey Man was real. Up until the age of 13 I was convinced that he lived in the dilapidated wood shed in my Grandparents back yard that neither I nor any of my cousins would dare venture into even if it offered the best possible place of seclusion in the entire neighborhood for a game of hide & seek. My God-Daddy had become old and too weak to tend to the shed, subsequently it would go winter after winter without maintenance or organization and we would play around it summer after summer without going in it or wandering too close near it. To reinforce our fears, we soon began to notice objects pile up along the back and side of it like wheel barrels, tires, and old engine parts. The ground ivy grew thick, over and through the piles of junk and began to cover much it like some kind of vegetative canopy, to the point you could hardly recognize what was beneath it. My oldest cousin Flip would say- "There's snakes in there..." and we believed him. We also believed that our uncles knew that it was the Boogey Man's lair and that they themselves were afraid to go in there. As I got older I realized what the truth was; my uncles were just too lazy to deal with the clutter and once my God-Daddy had passed away, there was no man around the household to make them accountable for such things as yard work.

As we got older we realized that the Boogey Man was nonsense. That we had to replace our fears and anxieties with common sense and beliefs more rooted in reality. We also took a lesson from our uncles as to what can happen when able bodied men won't till the ground and shuck their responsibilities— things get out of control...

On December 14, 2012 a young man who's name I won't mention as it disgusts me to do so, who much like a bad weed himself, walked into a classroom of first graders carrying an assault rifle and choked the life out of 20 young budding children. He also took the life of his own mother and several other faculty and staff during the incident at the Sandy Hook Elementary School in Newtown Connecticut. The tragedy has sparked a national debate over gun control to which the Obama Administration has promised action. I can't say why it takes tragedies of these kinds of proportions to invoke a spiritual movement in this country focused on doing the right thing? For instance it took the bombing of a church in Alabama, and the loss of life of four innocent little girls to increase pressure on the U.S. Government to pass legislation (Civil Rights Act) to stop this kind of extremist violent behavior. One might think that preventing the unnecessary loss of human life would be motivation enough for a law maker, to act in good conscience and support any legislation that works toward achieving that goal. However, greed sets the precedent for the tone of conversation within Washington and thus the unnecessary loss of human life, for a law maker, has to be weighed out against the unnecessary loss of income from corporate lobbyist that he/she may be receiving under the table or as Newt Gingrich puts it- *Consulting Fees*. Thus there are factions within both parties who are able to shoot down any proposed gun legislation often times before it even completes a news cycle.

I heard Joe Scarborough on Chris Mathews Hardball the other evening speaking about the dilemma the G.O.P. is facing over this most recent gun issue. He made mention to how the conservative party had become so extreme that even hardcore conservatives like himself are no longer the center of his party. Instead extremists like Wayne LaPierre are now the new norm on the face of the political party which once held reasonable centrist views. I agree with Joe whole-heartedly on this issue. I'm just sorry it's taken him so long to realize that his party has been under siege by conservative fanatics for quite some time now. Fanatics who operate on the basis of perpetuating paranoia with *Boogey Man Politics* and playing on the raw emotions of the truly less informed. They are those who believe they are in indeed a part of God's Army who will one day be called to arms against the wicked federal government and as a result it is common practice for them to live by their guns.

As much as extremist groups hate the federal government, they hate the advancement of the other races, in particular the black race, equally as much. They believe through some twisted rational that the Federal Government is partial to blacks, that the government disrupted an otherwise perfect balance of master and slave harmony and therefore are to blame for all the perceived ills of society. You see to an extremist, having a nigger as a slave is not an illness, in fact they feel just the opposite, having a nigger in the White House is a sure sign that society has become diseased ridden and the only way to heal the nation is to pick up a gun and start killing. This is what paranoia does to the human psyche. It renders all concepts of rational thinking indigent and the only resolve an afflicted soul can derive at is in the death of his enemies. The attack on 911, by yet even more extremist, only exacerbated the fears of extremist here at home. Now their paranoia manifests on multiple levels:

- Federal Takeover

- Black Empowerment

- Terrorist Attacks by Muslims

- Gay Liberation

- Latino Immigration

At the heart of each of these levels of alienation is change, which the extremist is solely against. He doesn't want nor welcome change and is quite satisfied with the way things were before a black man could become president. To him, Obama is a radical Boogey Man hell bent on taking his gun away just in time for the *Revolution*. He's a doomsday prepper too which him and fellow associates urgently await the day that America falls into mass chaos and they can retreat to cornfield bunkers to fight the war on their terms.

The resistance the NRA has put up against gun reform is not about preserving a hunters right to use a bushmaster in order to bring down game. It's about preserving a philosophy that fundamentalists have adopted as a living doctrine. It is a philosophy rooted in concepts of White Supremacy, insurrection, and the use of violence as a means to an end. It feeds an industry which profits off the fear of the misinformed and the unwillingness of those who know better, to behave like adults. In an attempt to show how much of a common sense issue the matter of gun legislation is, Obama made an appeal to the nation while putting forth his gun legislation proposals along side of four 1st graders during a press conference. The children had written letters to the President which were filled with pleas for him to do something about guns and prevent the unnecessary loss of life of other children due to gun violence. Americas Bully –n-Chief jumped out in front of the press and accused the President of using the children as human shields, saying sarcastically that "You gotta do what the kids want, gotta answer all their letters to Santa Clause…" he further added that after seeing the children with Obama it would be very difficult to deny Obama's legislation proposals. I'm sorry Rush but the death of 20 children at the hand of a deranged kid wielding an assault rifle is more than enough to move most Americans to seek some kind of gun reform.

Recent polls show that 90% percent of Americans, including gun owners themselves, are in favor of universal background checks which the president strongly urges. Unfortunately, within the same context another 74% of those polled said that more armed security guards would help prevent mass shootings in public places which is exactly what Wayne LaPierre proposes. "This is why I say "White Folks Be Trip'n"; let us analyze this for a second. Mass shootings in the past few years or so have been carried out by deranged individuals possessing high tech semi-automatic weapons with clip capacities of 30 rounds each. In most cases they have been reported to have more fire power than the police who are initially called to the scene. In order to be effective against a perpetrator with this kind of weaponry an armed security guard would need to be better if not equally outfitted. He would not be able to carry this weapon discretely in a holster upon his hip. He would have to wield this weapon over his shoulder or in his hand in front of our children. They would see this every day and it would become their reality. I remember the first time I saw armed men with automatic weapons mixed in with the general public. I was on my honeymoon in Riviera Mya, Mexico walking the pavilion. I can recall the mixed emotions I felt looking at uniformed men carrying assault rifles right outside the café were my wife and I had chosen to have lunch. One part of me felt like it was a bit aggressive, but then the realization that I wasn't in the states anymore had set in and I came to grips with where I actually was at the time— the land of drug cartels and random kidnappings and armed men with assault rifles are just a par for the course. I dread thinking that this is where headed in American society.

We all have to get a grip one way or the other. No race of people is without its quarks or idiosyncrasies; we all have shortcomings in how we deal with one another when it comes to matters of race or cultural differences. However this extreme paranoia that white males in particular have, about being devoid of power is harmful to the forward progress and changing demographics of America and if we were to take it a step further, humanity. When the rest of the world looks at the U.S. in their backyards telling them how to be humane with one another, yet see us here at home killing each other in mass shootings and racially denigrating the President, it sends a contradicting statement around the world as to what right America truly has to tell others how to live. Dissension amongst Americans is bad for our global image. There is an obvious difference in *healthy debating* and *obstruction*. A good healthy debate over an issue or difference of opinion can lead to a better understanding of contrasting views and ultimately common ground. Obstruction leads to a lack of progress, breakdowns in communication and political stalemates in Washington to which no Government can function. The people see this and lose faith in their leaders; the future becomes dismal and bleak. When the youth get involved in politics as they have over the past two elections they're trying to tell us something. Perhaps that if you adults can't get this done and have sensible conversations in this country about how to move the nation forward then we'll have to do it for you. After all we're the ones who have to inherit this mess.

SUMMARY

Despite an enormous amount of opposition, Obama managed to put some significant achievements under his belt going into his second term. I know many of us were expecting him to rush in like the "Fix it up Chappie" and whisk all of our problems away, but in the end it's really up to the citizens to make mature, responsible decisions in order to change the course of direction within society. I heard David Brooks on Meet the Press tell David Gregory one Sunday that "Obama always governs like a visitor from a morally superior planet." Well, immensely immoral times like these calls for men and women of great moral esteem to come forward. We need them to remind us that 20 children gunned down at the onset of their lives is wrong, that a young man who's profiled and gunned down while walking home with a bag of skittles in hand is wrong, that a young woman persecuted by a national media mogul for speaking out about birth control is wrong, that millions of Americans facing foreclosure because big banks decided to gamble with their mortgages is wrong, that discriminating against gay men and women in our nation's armed forces is wrong. What is a true leader if one cannot be an example of good moral character to his followers? Perhaps Brooks would find more comfort living under the fine examples of moral leadership shown to us by Raul Castro, Bashar al-Assad or Islam Karimov. Certainly, no one wants to live under a tyranny, which Right Wing media and Conservative extremist accuse this president of perpetrating every day. I tend to laugh at assertions like these because they can hardly be taken seriously. What I do take seriously is consideration for the type of world I want to raise my children in. I remember how proud I was when Barack was elected and for the first time in my life I felt like the playing field had somewhat been leveled for them. All those things I thought were impossible had in fact become possible and the sky was the limit for anything they wanted to be in life. It's the kind of inspiration young boys and girls need of all races and backgrounds. It's the kind of value that we should all want to encourage. Indeed it is change, positive change, and nothing that any of us should fear. However, in the last four years I've watched and listened as extreme values and agendas took center stage in American politics. I've seen guns at political rallies and finger pointing in the face of the President. Perhaps most disturbing is the dog whistling that arose out of the 2012 campaign along with the effort to suppress the vote in the minority community. It seemed as if bad men would stop at nothing to keep good things from happening in America. So I watched for months on end, the election cycle of presidential nominees during the 2012 campaign season. I watched often times in disgust over the things I heard, especially after telling my children that we had come so far. But something happened this time around— yes, something happened with even more profound significance than the first time it had happened. This time a coalition of people came together and rallied behind Obama, not to make history, but to reinforce the values that make this country great in the first place, values of equality, fairness, and opportunity.

The year 2012 will go down in history as the year America made a stand against corporate interests to buy and sell elections and rebelled against House Republicans that would hold this nation's economy hostage in order to push a political agenda. We coalesced around the notion that we're all in this together and that no man is an island whether he be rich or poor. We signified through our vote that we would not abandon our seniors, trivialize women's issues, or dampen the hopes of immigrants all over this nation. We will not persecute those in the LGBT community and we absolutely will not condone the blatant acts of racial divide and conquer politics in this country. We're not going to reward companies for shipping jobs overseas; we want those jobs back here on American soil and above all else, we're not going to appeal Obama Care.

So with a sigh of relief, this time I was able to tell my children that the American voter made all the difference in the outcome of the 2012 election. That one day soon they too will have the obligation to preserve the rights of others to vote just as the current generation did for them. I mentioned earlier that great leaders must have vision and should be able to sell that vision to others in hopes of making it a reality for all. I see the vision that Obama has for this nation and fully support it. It's the same vision that 51% of the voter electorate have chosen to aspire towards in the next four years under Obama's leadership. As Barack's vision begins to crystallize, I see young people at the center of it all leading the world as scholars, engineers, scientist or athletes competing at the next World Olympics Games. I see a vision of a nation where young men and women are proud to be United States soldiers led by a Commander and Chief who they know would not put them in harm's way based on a hunch or gut feeling. With such a defined vision for America's future, the work of revolution can begin. It already has in a lot of cases where young people, free to express themselves, are pioneers in innovations such as Facebook and Twitter which connect the world in an instant with a click. We must continue to provide a progressive environment healthy enough for their ideas to flourish, where they can take on the challenges of tomorrow by tackling climate change or make breakthroughs on renewable energy sources. Once during a lecture in an American History class I took while attending Wayne State University, I learned that there's a big difference between a president and a *Great President*. We've had 44 presidents but only a handful of Great Presidents. Does Obama have the ability to join the ranks of the Great Ones? Will he successfully tackle the issues of the day like balancing the budget, passing true immigration reform, improve upon our safety net for seniors, or rebuild our nation's crumbling infrastructure? Can he tackle gun legislation and end mass shootings in America? Can he implement high speed rail? Perhaps the biggest challenge facing our nation is the need for someone to lay the foundation for a new *technological revolution* in America— a framework for which our nation can make the strides necessary to become the leaders of tomorrow's technological industry which would be a true testament to Obama's legacy.

Obama's idea of a level playing field, health care for all, and an America on the cutting edge of technological advancements doesn't coincide with the vision of endless wars and spiritual crusades in the name of democracy that Right Wing Conservatives have envisioned for our nation's future. Based upon the last couple of decades it would appear as though Republican leadership would ordain the use of our nation's military in order to police the entire world in the hunt for criminals and international tyrants, while forcefully indoctrinating smaller countries with American values. They use cutting edge technology in the form of weapons to subjugate weaker nations rather than explore its uses in medical breakthroughs or energy conservation. It is the epitome of misplaced values and speaks to the heart of the fear element discussed in chapter 8, that white males feel threatened by the social advancements of other non-white societies.

Lockheed Martin isn't concerned with World Peace. Global conflict brings with it tremendous opportunity for weapons manufacturers to profit from destruction and international construction companies to profit through the process of rebuilding nations ravished by war. Because Obama is not a War Pig, his agenda conflicts with those in power who have the ability to manufacture war for the sake of profit, making him an easy target for conspirators. Let us not assume for one minute that conflict between nations' only occurs when two or more parties disagree. We have to take in to consideration the fact that weapons with no target have no value and those that manufacture weapons are among the biggest lobbyist in Washington. Their investors expect profits and returns on their dividends no matter how revered the Peace Prize Winner or vocal the Anti-War Protester.

Obama's challenge in the next four years is not to bolster the Arab Spring or referee Israeli and Palestinian conflict. There is a much more challenging task at hand in convincing paranoid radicals to set aside their fears of being rendered powerless in the new world and convince them of the power to be gain from solving the more complex broader issues like climate change, poverty, or universal health care.

Obama is Dangerous for America not because of his ideologies or resolve to take on the bigger challenging issues; he's a threat to those who see traditional white supremacy as the most picturesque view of American social hierarchy. He embodies a movement that in essence disqualifies the normalcy in America that white males are the most adept to lead a nation as sovereign as the United States. His presence in the White House reinforces the notion that strong leadership takes many forms and is not a rite of passage and it tells the children of the world to dream bigger than ever before.

The danger I speak of is not from Obama directly but rather indirectly as those who see Obama's presidency as the beginning decline of western civilization will stop at nothing to rid themselves of this god awful omen. The legitimacy of the potential dangers of this president's demise must be taken seriously as perhaps now more than ever America is on the cusp of immense social changes. As I have pointed out throughout this work, the opposition to this president has been of unprecedented proportions and will continue so long as the potential exists that any other minority or woman could be the next president of the United States.

Perhaps when the term American means the same thing for all citizens within this nation, Obama will be accepted and the notion that he is dangerous for America will be rejected. But so long as Americans deem it necessary to classify groups of different ethnic backgrounds within this country as African-American, Latin-American, Asian-American, Native-American, or anything other than just plain ole' Americans, those that see themselves as the only true Americans will sacrifice everything in order to preserve what they believe to be at the core of traditional American social autonomy; white male leadership.

GOD BLESS THE UNITED STATES OF AMERICA

www.ingramcontent.com/pod-product-compliance
Lightning Source LLC
Chambersburg PA
CBHW071734020426
42331CB00008B/2033